Lenawee County and the Civil War

Ray Lennard

The History Press

Published by The History Press
Charleston, SC
www.historypress.net

Cover: Flag in the collection of the Lenawee County Historical Museum, photograph by Amanda Ebbutt.

First published 2016

Manufactured in the United States

ISBN 978.1.46713.552.8

Library of Congress Control Number: 2016937195

Contents

Acknowledgements

This work would not have been possible without the assistance from several people and institutions. The Lenawee County Historical Society in Adrian and the Hudson Museum provided a wealth of information during the research phase of the project. A special thank-you to Mike Mills and Hazel Monahan of the Hudson Museum for their assistance and their dedication to preserving the rich past of our area. The staff of the Bentley Historical Library at the University of Michigan provided access to the rich collections of Michigan history housed in the institution and quickly answered repeated requests. Chuck Harpst at the Tecumseh District Library went above and beyond in his assistance in tracking down Tecumseh-based information. Noelle Keller was very generous in sharing her time and the resources held in the collection at the Shipman Library at Adrian College.

My reenacting "family" was great in answering queries at all hours of the day and night. Brian Crater assisted in tracking down information and acting as a sounding board when I was stuck. Both Gary Holmes and Marty Bertera have endlessly researched local soldiers and the units that they served in, providing a wealth of information. Bob Elliott provided both information and encouragement throughout this project.

Lindsey Sanford and Amanda Ebbutt both deserve a special thank-you, as they spent endless hours reading and rereading passages of the manuscript for errors and context. Amanda took time out of her schedule to aid in photography when I needed assistance.

Acknowledgements

I am deeply indebted to Krista Slavick at the The History Press for answering random questions quickly and for helping me weave through the publishing process.

Lastly, this book would not have been possible without Kara Lennard. Without her support and motivation, this book would never have been finished.

Introduction

Will Carleton, born on October 21, 1845, just east of Hudson, became Michigan's poet laureate. The young Will showed aptitude in school, and his parents allowed him to continue his education at Hillsdale College. While in school, Carleton worked in newspapers as an editor and writer. Honing his poetry skills, Carleton submitted a poem about marital problems to the *Toledo Blade* in 1871, and it was published. *Harper's* magazine picked up the poem, and the twenty-five-year-old became a household name overnight. Will would publish eleven books and countless other individual works of poetry.

During the Civil War, Carleton's brother Henry enlisted in the Eighteenth Michigan Infantry, Company A. Henry would be captured in Athens, Alabama, and imprisoned in Cahaba Prison. While in the camp, Henry Carleton contracted an illness and died on March 23, 1865.

After the war, the Carleton family traveled to Alabama in an attempt to locate the burial site of Henry and return the bones back to Michigan. The search was unsuccessful.

Carleton often returned to the subject of the Civil War dead in his poetry. In "Cover Them Over for Decoration Day" in his 1871 book *Poems*, one can feel the loss of a brother mourning for his sibling. Carleton writes:

Cover the face that motionless lie,
Shut from the blue of the glorious sky;
Faces once decked with the smiles of the gay,
Faces now marked by the frown of decay.

Eyes that looked friendship and love to your own,
Lips that the thoughts of affection made known;
Brows you have soothed in the hour of distress,
Cheeks you have brightened by tender caress.
Oh how they gleamed at the nation's first cry!
Oh how they streamed when they bade you good-by!
Oh how they glowed in the battle's fierce flame!
Oh how they paled when the death-angel came!
Cover them over, O cover them over,
Parent and husband and brother and lover!
Kiss in your hearts those dead heroes of ours,
And cover them over with beautiful flowers!

Hundreds of men left Lenawee County to serve in the American Civil War; some returned home, while others are buried in southern soil. The response to the war effort should surprise no one given the popularity of antislavery and the Underground Railroad in the county prior to the war. The following work highlights the efforts taken by men and women to bring an end to slavery and preserve the Union.

1

Prelude to the War

While no one can agree on the exact origins of the Civil War, it is clear that the practice of slavery was one of the key causes. In the 1820s, national events involving slavery may have seemed far away for the first settlers of Lenawee County focusing on establishing a community, but they became a focal point for conversations in the county. These conversations created actions locally that had an impact on events on the national stage. From the formation of antislavery groups that advocated for universal education to the establishment of political groups that still exist today, Lenawee County's participation in the abolitionist movement translated into an active and influential role before and during the American Civil War.

Small settlements were springing to life in the areas that would be known as Adrian, Tecumseh and Hudson, and the pioneers of newly founded Lenawee County brought with them interests, values and ideas from the more settled regions of New England from whence they hailed. One of those ideas that spread to the frontier was the antislavery movement. While it could trace its roots back to the Quaker Church, debates over the morality of the practice of slavery and the idea of a rapid end to slavery resonated in the Old Northwest Territory, and consequently, antislavery groups sprung up in Ohio and spread into Michigan and beyond.

In Lenawee County, the antislavery movement quickly became an integral part of community life, starting as small pockets of individuals who shared similar ideas first seeking to interact on the frontier. As the movement grew in popularity and membership, education was deemed to be vital in bringing an end to slavery. In the 1840s and '50s, abolitionist forces viewed politics as a means to end the practice of slavery, and leaders emerged working at the local, state and national levels. When events converged that threatened to dissolve the Federal government over the issue of slavery in 1861, hundreds of men from Lenawee County stepped forward to serve in the armies of the Union.

The efforts of people such as Elizabeth Chandler, Laura Haviland, Charles Croswell and Asa Mahan as participants in the antislavery movement show how the movement grew and transformed the residents of Lenawee into active participants in the Civil War.

BEGINNINGS OF A MOVEMENT

Elizabeth Margaret Chandler established the Logan Female Anti-Slavery Society. Hailing from Philadelphia, Pennsylvania, Elizabeth came to Lenawee County with her aunt Ruth Evans and brother Thomas Chandler. She was well known in the Quaker Church and in antislavery circles in Philadelphia.

At the age of nine, Elizabeth began a budding career in writing. In 1823, at age sixteen, her first work was published. Her writing focused on poetry for the antislavery movement, in which she attempted to make the point that anyone touched by the plight of the slaves must do something to help. In the Philadelphia area, this meant signing petitions to call for the end of slavery. While women like Elizabeth Chandler could not vote, and therefore could not sign the petition, they could circulate the petitions and advocate for their spouses and male family members to sign.

In the 1820s, Chandler started working with Benjamin Lundy, authoring articles, poems and columns for Lundy's antislavery paper, *Genius of Universal Emancipation*. While contributing to the *Genius*, Chandler became acquainted with William Lloyd Garrison, who worked as an editor for the paper. Chandler and Lundy maintained correspondence on a regular basis.

When Elizabeth Chandler arrived in Lenawee County with her brother and aunt, she found herself among friends in a Quaker community. Darius Comstock (the father of Addison Comstock, who would start a town that became known as Adrian) was a neighbor of Elizabeth. In discussions of current events, Elizabeth found that "Uncle Darius" (as she called him) and the Comstock family loathed the practice of slavery.

Miss Chandler also stayed connected to Philadelphia through regular correspondence with the family members who remained behind. Among the

Elizabeth Chandler came to Lenawee County in 1830. Two years later, she formed an antislavery society in Raisin Township that continued on after her death. *Courtesy of Bentley Historical Library, University of Michigan.*

news of daily life on the East Coast, the letters to Elizabeth included news on William Lloyd Garrison's libel trial, free black activities in Philadelphia and other items that piqued her interest in the evils of slavery.

Finding herself among like-minded neighbors, such as the Comstocks, and with a support network on the East Coast, Elizabeth Chandler set out in 1832 to organize a women's antislavery society in her new neighborhood. She named it Logan Female Anti-Slavery Society after the town of Logan (which would become Adrian). It is considered the first women's antislavery society established in the Old Northwest Territory. Elizabeth's aunt Ruth noted the event in a letter to her sister Jane Howell, sent on October 22, 1832:

> *Through Elizabeth's influence, we have established an antislavery society here. Our first meeting was held at the house two weeks ago. They are to be monthly. We suppose there will be about twelve new members at our next meeting. They heartily meet with it, though many have seldom heretofore thought much on the subject.*[1]

Chandler would get the organization started, but by the spring of 1834, she had come down with a fever that would not go away. After a long period of illness, Elizabeth Chandler died on November 2, 1834, at the age of twenty-seven. She left behind an impressive collection of poems, letters and essays that spoke against the practice of slavery in America. As a legacy, Chandler set in motion significant antislavery activities in Philadelphia and Lenawee County. As proof of her importance, William Lloyd Garrison published notice of her death in his paper, *The Liberator.* When Garrison visited Adrian

In April 2014, a group of Adrian College students led by Reverend Chris Momany worked with local agencies to revamp the burial ground where Chandler was interred. The site is located off Breckel Highway in Adrian. *Photo by Kara Lennard.*

in 1853 to lecture at an antislavery rally, he took time to visit the grave of his old acquaintance Chandler to pay tribute to her leadership.

In 1834, the Logan Female Anti-Slavery Society took a giant step forward. On a national level, the formation of the American Antislavery Society allowed local abolitionist groups to organize under a national umbrella organization. Led by William Lloyd Garrison, the American Antislavery Society allowed small local groups to share ideas and pool resources to end slavery. The Logan Female Anti-Slavery Society was one of the first two auxiliaries to this national group.

In Raisin Township, 1834 marked the year that a few Quakers of the area decided the issue of slavery was so important that they had to withdraw from the more conservative Quakers. Nearly twenty Quakers left the local church, including Laura Smith Haviland; her husband, Charles; her father, Daniel Smith (who had been a minister in the Quaker community for almost thirty years); and her mother, Sene Smith (who had been an elder in the community for nearly as long). The Havilands and Smiths would go on to have a major impact on the antislavery movement over the next two decades.

Why did they leave? Simply put, they felt they could do more to end slavery. Perhaps it was Laura Haviland's membership in the Logan Female Anti-Slavery Society and the writings of Elizabeth Chandler, with the theme of actively working to help those enslaved, that precipitated their leaving the Quaker church.

In 1837, Charles and Laura Haviland opened a manual-labor school at their home. The school's goal was assisting children housed in Lenawee County's poorhouse by teaching them domestic skills. Girls would be taught housework, sewing and knitting by Laura Haviland. Boys worked with Charles Haviland, learning farming techniques. In teaching vocational skills, the Havilands hoped to break the poverty cycle, equipping their students with marketable skills. The school would fail financially because Lenawee governmental leaders would not provide financial aid; however, the Havilands saw the promise of the school and came up with a grander idea.

The Havilands proposed that their school take up the challenge extended by the Michigan Antislavery Society to provide educational opportunities to African Americans along with whites. No such school in Michigan existed, and there were few examples in America. In 1839, the Raisin Institute open its doors to all. An October 23, 1839 advertisement in the *Michigan Freeman* stated:

Laura Haviland showing some of the tools of the slave owner: chains and other forms of bondage found on a Louisiana plantation. Haviland worked throughout her life for social reforms. *Courtesy of the Lenawee County Historical Society.*

> *A manual labor school is about going into operation in Raisin, Lenawee County, Michigan, six miles east of Adrian. A male and female teacher are on the premises, and will begin their regular labors on the first of November . . . the table will be furnished with a vegetable diet, at from 50 to 75 cents per week. Room rent 12½ cents per week. Instruction 25 cents per week. Those wishing to erect small buildings for themselves can receive board and tuition at above rates.*[2]

The school did well by all accounts. Laura Haviland's brother Harvey Smith was instrumental in getting the school up and running. Smith provided the capital to start the school by selling his 160-acre farm and investing the proceeds from the sale into constructing buildings that housed nearly fifty students. The principals and educators of the school came from Oberlin College—the new, integrated liberal arts college near Cleveland, Ohio, run by Asa Mahan. Mahan's radically liberal views on abolition had an impact on his graduates, and they carried new views on ending slavery to Lenawee County.

With new facilities and strong teachers, the school quickly earned a reputation for quality. The school roster usually had a handful of black students. Haviland hoped for greater African American enrollment, but their presence helped to end any prejudices of the fellow white students. Haviland cited one such example in her book *A Woman's Life Work:*

> *A young lady from Jackson County . . . was brought to us by her father to become qualified for teaching. But her sensibilities were so shocked at meeting in her grammar class a colored man that she returned to her room weeping over her disgrace, and resolved to write her father to come and take her home immediately . . . and while waiting for her father to take her from this "nigger school" (as she and many others called it), a letter came from him advising her to remain. . . . She soon became reconciled, and before a half-term closed, when she threatened to leave at all events (as she read her father's letter), she came to that colored man to assist her in intricate parsing lessons. Before the close of the first term she as frequently applied to James Martin, her colored classmate, for assistance in solving difficult problems in mathematics as to the others.*[3]

Impressively, Haviland reported that the local community did not react in a negative manner toward her interracial school.

While the Havilands and Smiths' school grew in Raisin Township, other areas of Lenawee County organized against slavery. By the late 1830s, the antislavery movement had gathered momentum in all areas of Lenawee County. The southeastern corner of the county, especially the Blissfield area, shows us the best example of the social movement's rapid growth. In a letter to Thomas Chandler (brother of Elizabeth Chandler, now serving as a local chairman in an abolitionist group), Hervey Bliss named the forty-three members of the Blissfield Antislavery Society. The names included such notable families of the Blissfield area as the Carpenters, Blisses, Kedzies and Giles. The list also named eighteen women, showing that this movement started by Elizabeth Chandler in Lenawee County would be led by women as well as men.[4]

ANTISLAVERY MOVEMENT BECOMES MAINSTREAM

Abolition forces at the state level organized in 1836 with the meeting of the Michigan State Antislavery Society. To bring about the end of slavery, this group called for moral persuasion and education on the issue rather than resorting to violence. It was also agreed that political action and legislation would be an ideal way to end slavery.

In 1841, Joel Carpenter of Blissfield and Paul Tabor of Adrian called for all those concerned about slavery to meet in Adrian for a convention. During the meeting, the group nominated Tabor (a staunch abolitionist) to run for state senate. Reverend Henry Tripp of Franklin Township received a nomination for a statehouse seat, along with Stephen Allen of Madison Township and William Kedzie of Deerfield. All of the men ran on the ticket of the Liberty Party, a single-issue political party devoted to ending slavery. While the men would not win, the precedent of running for office on the platform of ending slavery had been set.

For the next several years, antislavery leaders in Lenawee ran for offices under the banners of the Liberty Party and, later, the Free Soil Party. Some political leaders in the community shared Addison J. Comstock's view when he stated that he was an antislavery supporter but felt the third-party candidates had no chance of victory. In 1854, several antislavery men from around the state met in Jackson, Michigan, to discuss the formation of a new political party. At the statewide meeting were Lenawee residents Fernando Beaman and Charles Croswell.

The meeting was in reaction to the Kansas-Nebraska Act, which allowed territories to decide if they were to be free states or allow slavery.

Fernando Cortez Beaman was the city attorney for Adrian when he attended the "Under the Oaks" meeting in Jackson that organized the Republican Party. Running as a Republican candidate, Beaman would go on to serve as Lenawee County's U.S. representative during the Civil War. *Courtesy of the Library of Congress.*

Many felt that this act modernized slavery and would cause it to spread across the North American continent. The newly minted Republican Party in Michigan drew up a thirteen-plank platform that called for the end of slavery, repeal of the Fugitive Slave Act and economic reforms. Remnants of the Liberty Party and the Free-Soil Party pledged to support Republican candidates. In the November elections, Republican candidates did what Liberty Party, Free-Soil Party and other antislavery parties could not do: won seats in local, state and national races.

The "Under the Oaks" meeting that formed the Republican Party also propelled the political careers of the two Lenawee County residents, Beaman and Croswell.

Born in New York, Beaman relocated to Manchester, Michigan, in 1838 and in 1840 moved to Tecumseh, where he worked as a lawyer. By 1843, Beaman had been appointed prosecuting attorney for Lenawee County. With the appointment, he relocated to Adrian.

Once in Adrian, Beaman became acquainted with Thomas Cooley. Thomas Cooley was a fellow lawyer, a founder of the Michigan branch of the Free-Soil Party and a published author of antislavery poems and essays. Together they opened a law office in Adrian. In 1856, the well-liked Beaman easily won election for mayor of Adrian.

In 1860, Fernando Beaman ran for the second congressional seat in the U.S. House of Representatives. He easily won the election and served in Congress from March 4, 1861, through March 3, 1871, representing Lenawee County throughout the Civil War. Perhaps the highlight of his term of office was his "yes" vote for the Thirteenth Amendment, which formally abolished slavery on January 31, 1865.

Daniel Hicks moved to Adrian with his nephew Charles M. Croswell in 1837. During the day, the twelve-year-old Charles Croswell worked as a carpenter, and at night he studied the law. In 1846, Croswell received an appointment to the position of deputy clerk. Croswell became interested in public office and in 1848 ran for the slot of county clerk on the Whig ticket, without success. Two years later, he successfully ran for the office of register of deeds on the Whig ticket.

In 1854, Charles Croswell served as the secretary for the "Under the Oaks" meeting that formed the Republican Party. Locally, he is known for organizing the investors to construct the Union Opera House, now known as Croswell Opera House, built during the Civil War. *Courtesy of the Lenawee County Historical Society.*

In 1855, Croswell joined the legal office formed by Thomas Cooley and Fernando Beaman. He went on to be appointed Adrian's city attorney in 1862 and, later in the year, was elected mayor of Adrian. Not satisfied with local office, Croswell ran for a seat in the Michigan senate, winning the election in the fall of 1862. He served three terms in the Michigan senate, serving as president pro tempore from 1863 through 1867.

The election of Croswell on the Republican ticket meant that abolitionists in Lenawee County had an ally in Lansing. In 1863, Croswell delivered an impassioned speech supporting Abraham Lincoln's Emancipation Proclamation and the president's handling of the Civil War. Croswell worked diligently in the Michigan senate in 1865 to oversee the ratification of the Thirteenth Amendment.

ON THE PATH TO CONFLICT: ABOLITIONISM IN LENAWEE IN THE 1850S

As the antislavery movement in the 1850s expanded in the world of politics, it redoubled its efforts to educate the public. Laura Smith Haviland was a leader in educating the public about the evils of slavery and in self-improvement. Her Raisin Institute had been open since 1839, and by 1850, the temporary buildings that had been erected were worn out. Laura Haviland and her staff set out to build a new campus while closing the old one. It took six years to finish the new schoolhouse. In 1857, Haviland was offered a $2,000 building for a fraction of the cost (only $300). She happily had the building moved the one mile to the Raisin Institute campus, where it served as the men's hall. With the new buildings on campus, the school's enrollment topped over two hundred students.

Haviland's school served as inspiration for another school in Lenawee County. The Woodstock Manual Labor Institute would open one mile north of Addison in 1846. Its founder, Prior Foster, was a free black from Ohio who had tried for years to open a school in other places. In Lenawee County, he found support for his school that taught vocational skills to blacks.

The staff of the Woodstock Manual Labor Institute was all black, a first in the state. In addition, when the school opened, only black students were admitted. It was not until 1848 that the school became integrated. Students from the northwest corner of Lenawee were attracted to the school thanks

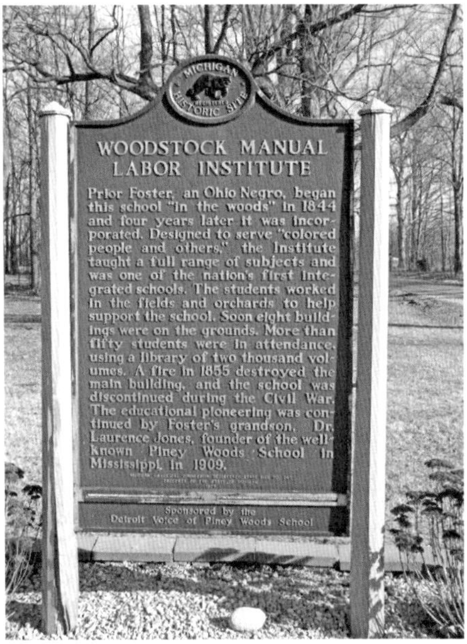

Above: A 1960s view of the last remaining building of the Woodstock Manual Labor Institute. Thanks to a strong antislavery population and well-to-do benefactors in Lenawee County, the vocational school operated from the 1840s up to the outbreak of the Civil War. *Courtesy of the Lenawee County Historical Society*.

to the quality of education and the variety of classes offered. The school stayed open up to the outbreak of the Civil War.

In the county seat of Adrian, another school was in the works just west of the city center. The work of three people—John McEldowney, Asa Mahan and Langford Berry—brought Adrian College into existence.

In 1854, in Leoni, Michigan, a Wesleyan theological seminary attempted to open under the leadership of John McEldowney. McEldowney left the Episcopal Church over the issue of slavery, relocating from Allegany, New York, to Michigan. McEldowney found a spiritual home in the Michigan Conference of the Methodist Episcopal Church.

John McEldowney served as president of the Michigan Union College when it was relocated to Adrian. At Adrian College, McEldowney worked first as a professor and then as the college president from 1864 to 1866. *Courtesy of Shipman Library, Adrian College.*

The Leoni Theological Institute opened thanks to a partnership with the Michigan Union College in Leoni, located southeast of Jackson, Michigan. The class of 1854–55 had eight students taught by three professors. Such a small student body created a financial bind for the institution almost immediately. Community support waned, and McEldowney sought out greener pastures for the fledgling college.

Drawn by the strong antislavery sentiments in the area, Asa Mahan came to Jackson, Michigan, in 1855. Forced out as president of Oberlin College in August 1850, Mahan traveled to Michigan seeking employment. Mahan's first job in Michigan was as pastor of the First Congregational Church in Jackson. While working there, he occasionally spoke at the Michigan Union College and became acquainted with

McEldowney. By 1857, Mahan had relocated to Adrian to work at the Plymouth Congregational Church.

When news of Leoni's financial strain reached Mahan, he saw this as an opportunity to not only move the college to Adrian but also to reenter the world of academia. The institution would bring prestige to the city of Adrian, and Mahan relished the idea of getting back into teaching after being dismissed from both Lane Seminary and Oberlin College.

Mahan entered into a race against Jackson for Adrian to become the home of Leoni Institute. Leaders in Jackson felt secure in the fact that they were closest to Leoni; the move would be mere miles. Mahan knew Adrian was larger than Jackson and richer by far. Mahan upped the ante in January 1859. At a meeting of local citizens at the Bidwell Hall on January 31, 1859, he proposed that the citizens of Adrian raise $30,000 to influence the move to their city.

A committee of citizens was elected at a mass meeting in early February. The committee, led by Langford Berry, went to work to garner support for the college. Berry, a local banker, decided the best course of action was to sell subscriptions for the college; a $100 subscription or more would entitle the investor to a vote for the election of six local trustees and a vote for the selection of a site in Adrian. Investors snapped up the shares, and by March, the $30,000 had been raised. The local trustees elected included Berry; probate judge Henry Hart, William H Scott, Esquire; Dr. Daniel K. Underwood (local pharmacist); Fernando Beaman; and Elihu L. Clark (an insurance salesman considered to be the richest man in Adrian).

With the funds secured, the trustees selected twenty acres of land along Madison Avenue, half located in Adrian Township and half in Madison Township. The land was donated by Berry and Underwood. The trustees authorized the construction of two buildings, North and South Halls, at a cost of $60,000. On March 29, 1859, the trustees drew up the Articles of Association and selected Asa Mahan to be the first president of the institution. Adrian College was born.[5]

The college became affiliated with the Wesleyan Methodist Church but would admit locals irrespective of religious affiliations. Students of all races and genders would be welcome as well. In the first year of operation, 212 students, including 78 women, took classes. Asa Mahan strongly believed in abolition and that education could be obtained by anyone, just as Raisin Institute and Woodstock Manual Labor Institute touted.

Adrian College, with Asa Mahan at the helm, attracted students who fully supported antislavery views. One former student, Dr. Loretta Mann

Reverend Asa Mahan was an outspoken proponent of education for all and for ending slavery. His unyielding beliefs often had him at odds with superiors. Mahan would lose his son Theodore, who served with the Sixteenth Michigan Infantry, at the Battle of Fredericksburg. *Courtesy of Shipman Library, Adrian College.*

Hammond (class of 1864), wrote to Adrian College president Harlan Feeman in 1935 stating that she attended Adrian College because of its strong abolitionist views.[6] The best example of the "radical positions" taken up by Mahan and his students came from the Star Literary Society. The group debated the activities of abolitionist John Brown and his raid on the Federal armory at Harpers Ferry, Virginia. The student group found that John

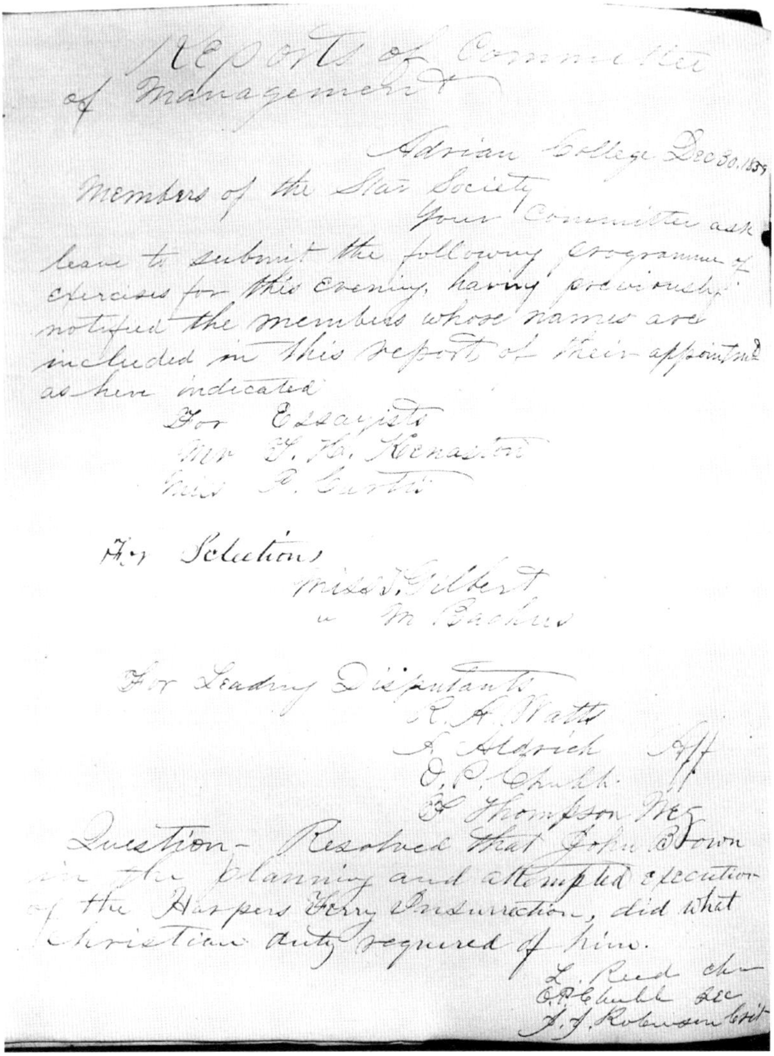

Reports of Committee of Management

Adrian College Dec 30. 1859

Members of the Star Society

Your Committee ask leave to submit the following programme of exercises for this evening, having previously notified the members whose names are included in this report of their appointment as here indicated

For Essayists
Mr F. H. Kenaston
Miss P. Curtis

For Selections
Miss I. Gilbert
" M. Backus

For Leading Disputants
R. A. Watts
A. Aldrich Aff
O. P. Chubb "
F. Thompson Neg

Question- Resolved that John Brown in the planning and attempted execution of the Harpers Ferry Insurrection, did what Christian duty required of him.

L. Reed chr
O. P. Chubb sec
A. J. Robinson crit

The December 30, 1859 minutes of the Star Literary Society, notable because students debated the John Brown Harpers Ferry raid. The group concluded that John Brown had done what Christian duty required of him in the attempted execution of the raid. *Courtesy of Shipman Library, Adrian College.*

Brown was morally right and "did what Christian duty required of him." What was once viewed as a radical belief had become more "mainstream" in Lenawee County thanks to the growth of antislavery groups.

ASSISTANCE TO FUGITIVES

One aspect of Lenawee County's antislavery history that always fascinates residents is the assistance provided to fugitive slaves by members of the Underground Railroad network. It is true that members of the antislavery societies did provide assistance to slaves fleeing their owners in the South. However, it was not a collection of hidden rooms, tunnels and cryptic signs and symbols; rather, it was a network of individuals committed to assisting with food, housing, education and finances. Fugitive slaves who entered Lenawee County found themselves in an area with strong abolitionists and an antislavery sentiment ingrained in the everyday lives of residents.

A prime example is the assistance Charles and Laura Haviland provided to Elise Hamilton and her free black husband, Willis. In the mid-1830s, Elise ran away from her owner, Dr. John Chester, when she discovered that he was considering selling her to the Deep South, an act that would move her away from her husband and children. The Hamiltons fled, and after spending some time in southern Indiana, they felt unsafe and relocated north to Michigan. Seeking a Quaker community where they knew they could find support, they arrived in Raisin Township.

Charles and Laura Haviland set out to help the fugitive Elise and her free husband. They took the Hamiltons in, and Charles arranged to have ten acres of his land set aside for the the Hamiltons to farm. The Hamiltons lived happily for three years until Elise became frightened of a stranger she presumed to be a southerner. The Hamiltons moved on to a new location and eventually settled in Ypsilanti.

In 1845, Charles Haviland died. Learning of Laura Haviland's situation, the Hamiltons moved back to the area to help Laura with the school and farm. Elise, curious about the status of her children, had staff members of the Raisin Institute inquire of her husband's old master. Dr. Chester, Elise's master, learned of this and attempted to capture her by sending a letter purporting to be from Willis's old master claiming he wished to see Willis and Elise one last time before he died. He claimed to be ill and said the travel to Adrian would be too far. The letter asked if Elise and Willis would be willing to meet him in Toledo.

Laura Haviland was suspicious of the letter and the story. Haviland volunteered to go to Toledo first to check to see if the letter was legitimate. If the letter was indeed from Willis's old master, the Hamiltons could take the next train down. What Haviland found was Dr. John Chester and two associates pretending to be the former owner of Willis Hamilton. Haviland sent word to the Hamiltons in Adrian that there were three suspicious gentlemen in Toledo and that she would be accompanying them to Adrian.

While en route to Adrian on the train, Dr. Chester realized Haviland was on to them. They confronted Haviland and pulled a pistol on her, threatening her with violence if she continued to interfere with his property. A train conductor came upon the sight and warned Chester and his associates to back down. As the train slowed to enter Sylvania, the party jumped from the car. It was a good choice for Dr. Chester and his friends, as more than forty Underground Railroad operators were gathered at the depot and had pledged to do whatever it took to keep the fugitive slave safe.

In 1847, the Hamiltons had moved to Canada and away from the threat of Dr. Chester. Dr. Chester, infuriated by the actions of Laura Haviland and the Underground Railroad workers in Ohio and Michigan, offered a $3,000 bounty on Laura Haviland. In the 1850s, with the passage of the Fugitive Slave Act, Thomas Chester, John's son, attempted once more to locate Elise.

Thomas Chester contacted a lawyer in Adrian, Robert Beecher, seeking information and assistance in locating Elise. Beecher asked Chester to leave his office; if he were to help, it would ruin his practice. Beecher then let Haviland know that Chester was in town looking for a fugitive slave.

When Chester went to the federal court in Detroit to get a warrant for Elise's arrest as property under the Fugitive Slave Act, the Underground Railroad network snapped into action. The judge who issued the order let the leader of the free black community in Detroit know that there was a slave catcher in the area looking for Elise Hamilton. Word went out throughout southeastern Lower Michigan letting agents of the Underground Railroad know that a southerner had just left Detroit, and they should be alert for arrivals from Detroit at local depots. Thomas Chester left the area empty handed.

The story of Elise Hamilton shows how the Underground Railroad portion of the antislavery movement operated in Lenawee County. It was a network of conservative antislavery men and women like Robert Beecher and more radical leaders (like those outside the depot in Sylvania) willing to confront slave catchers working together to keep fugitives safe. It is also interesting to note that free blacks and fugitives lived openly in Lenawee County next door to whites.[7]

ELECTION OF 1860

The formation of the Republican Party in Jackson, Michigan, in 1854; the violence in Kansas in 1856; and the Dred Scott decision in the Supreme Court in 1857 made it clear that the question of slavery was front and center in the presidential election of 1860. The Republican Party showed its political power and the huge support it had garnered on November 2, 1860, in Adrian.

The rally showcased the emergence of a group within the Republican Party known as the Wide Awakes. The paramilitary political group consisted of young men who participated in marching formations, carrying torches while dressed in matching full robes or capes and black hats. The Wide Awakes marched to and from political speeches and rallies to show their support for the Republican candidates and rally others to the party.

On that November day in 1860, Adrian welcomed 80 Wide Awakes from Tecumseh, 78 from Manchester, 32 from Clinton, 47 from Napoleon, 60 from Hudson, 60 from Palmyra, 80 from Blissfield, 76 from Adrian Township and 60 from Rome—573 men who would march through the streets of Adrian. Joining the marchers were 30 mounted Wide Awakes (also known as Lincoln Rangers after candidate Abraham Lincoln) from Adrian, 84 from Adrian Township, 81 from Dover, 65 from Medina and 70 from Fairfield.

Besides the 903 Wide Awakes marching and mounted, there would also be 865 wagon teams from around the area coming into Adrian to see the speeches and participate in the parade. The parade was split into four sections, with groups marching from each direction on Main and Maumee Streets to the four corners of town and commencing their routes to the county fair grounds. That afternoon, it was estimated that 20,000 people gathered to hear the featured speaker, Cassius Clay, an antislavery orator from Kentucky. Adrian's population in 1860 was around 7,000, while the county had a population of nearly 40,000.[8]

After the speech and picnic, those gathered waited until nightfall for the torchlight parade that would weave around Adrian. Adding to the torchlights from the Wide Awakes were candles and lanterns placed in the windows of Republican-leaning homes and businesses.

Other towns in Lenawee hosted Republican rallies during the fall of 1860. Tecumseh saw two thousand people gather for a rally to hear Austin Blair, the Republican candidate for governor. Ridgeway, Macon and Morenci held similar but smaller rallies. It was clear that antislavery supporters wanted a political party at the national level to stand up to proslavery Southerners.

Just a few days after the rally in Adrian, the Republican Party won a great victory. Abraham Lincoln won at the national level. Locally, the Republicans did equally as well. Fernando Beaman successfully won a seat in Congress in a district that included Monroe and part of Detroit in Wayne County.

The stage was set for a great conflict between North and South with the secession of South Carolina. On December 20, 1860, South Carolina passed a resolution of secession and, in documents, cited the Northern states' refusal to return runaway slaves as a breakdown of the federal compact. Antislavery groups in Lenawee and beyond evolved from social gatherings and grew into a political juggernaut.

2

1861: War Comes to Lenawee

"Treason Begun!" reported the *Adrian Daily Expositor* on December 21, 1860, when South Carolina voted to leave the Union. The newspapers of Lenawee County followed closely the developments as Southern states ratified acts of secession. Both Democrats and Republicans of the area admonished the Southern states for attempting to break up the Union.

Some knew war was merely months away. Dwight D. Woodbury of Adrian wrote to the newly elected governor of Michigan in January 1861 offering the services of the state's Third Militia Regiment. Woodbury commanded the regiment and was a respected business leader in Adrian. He felt strongly that the militia of Michigan would be equal to any task that the Federal government asked of it.

The next four years proved Woodbury correct, as hundreds of men marched off from Lenawee County to all theaters of the bloody Civil War. Men from the cities of Adrian, Tecumseh, Hudson and the various townships around Lenawee found themselves in major battles, in small skirmishes, on guard duty and held as prisoners of war. Politicians worked at the state and local levels to ensure the Union would stand and that the war would end the practice of slavery in the United States. Civilians worked on the homefront to care and comfort the wounded, as well as manufacture war materiel and supply the war effort.

THE WAR COMES

The winds of war blew into Lenawee County on April 12, 1861, when Confederate forces in Charleston, South Carolina, fired on the Federal forces in Fort Sumter in Charleston Harbor. The thirty-four-hour bombardment of the fort stirred the emotions of everyone in Lenawee.

In Adrian, Charles Cleveland wrote in his diary that "the ball is opened . . . war is inaugurated."

Cleveland, a merchant in Adrian, penned a detailed diary before and during the war, painting a vibrant picture of the community. On April

Charles Cleveland operated a grocery and general merchandise store in Adrian. Throughout the Civil War years, Cleveland kept an extensive diary that highlighted the coming and going of troops, as well as other significant events in Lenawee County. *Courtesy of Bentley Historical Library, University of Michigan.*

14, he wrote, "Many of our young men express a strong desire to serve their country in this time of peril." The next day, local leadership of the Republican and Democratic Parties called for a meeting to discuss the national events at Bidwell Hall. Addison Comstock, the founder of Adrian, spoke at length about the need to defend the county from tyranny. Charles Croswell gave a speech arguing that the alternative to fighting was to see the county fall into anarchy.[9]

In the middle of the meeting, the organizers learned that there were hundreds of people outside Bidwell Hall wanting to hear the speeches. The meeting adjourned and relocated to the balcony of the Brackett House (owned by Dwight Woodbury), on the northeast corner of Maumee and Winter Streets. Here, on the impromptu podium, Colonel Woodbury stated that he and members of the local militia units were ready to march and put down this rebellion.

A postwar photograph of members of the Adrian Light Guard (circa 1890). William Humphrey (back row, far right) served in the Second Michigan from the start of the Civil War. R.B. Robbins (middle row, third from left) served in the Fourth Michigan Cavalry. D.D. Sinclair (middle row, fourth from left) worked in the Commissary Department and was an agent for the Pinkerton Agency after the war. *Courtesy of Lenawee County Historical Museum.*

Adrian had two local fraternal military organizations: the Adrian Guards and the Adrian Hardee Cadets. The Adrian Guards were the older organization, originally organized in 1834, when Ohio claimed the Toledo strip. While that disagreement passed without a bloody fight and would be settled in the courts, the Adrian Guards did equip themselves with muskets and cartridge boxes said to be from the time of General Lafayette, of Revolutionary War fame. By 1860, the Adrian unit had donned Zouave uniforms patterned after the famous French military units and attended statewide military drills to hone its skills.

The Adrian Hardee Cadets were a relatively new organization formed in September 1860 by Loren L. Comstock. The unit elected Comstock as captain, and he was charged with managing the nearly seventy members. The group dropped the name Hardee and became known simply as the Adrian Cadets.

The two military units offered their services to Governor Austin Blair. The Adrian Cadets were placed in the First Michigan Infantry. The Adrian Guards learned that they would become Company D in the Second Michigan Infantry. Dwight Woodbury, whose letter in January 1861 spoke of his willingness to lead Michigan troops against the Southern states, again offered his leadership services to the governor.

Woodbury had hoped to lead the First Michigan Regiment but was passed over. The governor did authorize Woodbury to open a recruiting office and gather one thousand men for service to the Federal government. Shortly thereafter, Woodbury received his appointment as colonel of the Fourth Michigan Regiment.

THE REACTION IN HUDSON

Hudsonites responded to the Civil War by holding a town hall meeting. The highlight of the meeting was the pledge of the Hudson Artillery (a local militia group formed in 1858) to serve the nation as volunteers to the Federal army. Led by fifty-two-year-old Ruben A. Beach, the eighty-member artillery group knew that if it volunteered, it would likely be accepted into service only as infantry. The town took up a collection at the end of the meeting (to assist in defraying the cost of outfitting the men), and in a few short minutes, over $700 was collected, according to the April 20, 1861 edition of the *Hudson Gazette*.

Albert Boies of Hudson joined the Hudson Zouave Cadets in April 1861. When the Fourth Michigan recruited in the area in the fall of 1861, Boies convinced his parents to allow him to join. Here, Boies is pictured in his Zouave Cadet uniform. *Courtesy of Hudson Museum.*

The men of the Hudson Artillery changed their moniker to the Lenawee Guards and soon found themselves placed in the Second Michigan as Company B. The members of Company B left Hudson in early May to join the rest of the regiment in Detroit. Before leaving, they received copies of the New Testament from Reverend L. Smith Hobart, and Captain Beach received a revolver.

Company B of the Second Michigan was not the only group to be organized in the spring of 1861. Samuel DeGolyer, a local politician and partner in a firm that manufactured wagon parts, worked to raise a company. DeGolyer wrote to Lansing seeking a place for his company, which he drilled every night. DeGolyer and his men soon received an appointment as Company F of the Fourth Michigan.

The zeal of war extended to the women of Hudson, as well. A committee was created to provide for soldiers' families while the men were off at war. The May 11 *Hudson Gazette* listed Mrs. A.L. Hill, Mrs. J.K. Boise, Mrs. Ingersoll, Mrs. S. DeGolyer, Mrs. M. Davis, Mrs. Ann Daniels, Mrs. Sornborger, Mrs. J. Rhodes, Mrs. Harriet Brown and Miss Julia Tracy as members of the group.

Even the youngest residents of Hudson worked to restore the Union. The May 11 edition of the *Hudson Gazette* reported:

> *The military spirit is now contagious. The juveniles of our village have caught it, and we now have two new companies, the first composed of boys from 12 to 16 years old, calling themselves the Hudson Zouave Cadets. They have regular drill and seem to be getting proficient at it. The other company consists of boys 6 to 10.*

The younger set soon focused on other pursuits, but the Zouave Cadets grew to a roster of thirty-eight members and maintained drill throughout the summer months of 1861.

FIRST MICHIGAN REGIMENT

Training in Detroit began on April 29 for the companies of the First Michigan Infantry. The Hardee Cadets from Adrian received the designation of Company K, with William Graves, from Adrian, as their captain. Loren Comstock of Adrian gained a promotion to the rank of lieutenant colonel. Two Adrian College students joined the Hardee Cadets in Detroit. Jerome H. Fee and Richard A. Watts both enlisted in the company for ninety days with the idea of a grand adventure in the summer and a return to the college to finish their degrees in the fall.

Officers in the unit had their hands full. Men from all walks of life were not used to the rigors and structure of military life. Most of the volunteers ignored the pleas of commanders for order and saw no use for drill, assuming that merely arriving on the field of battle would cause the Rebel forces to surrender. The ninety-day term of enlistment caused many to see no reason to become fully indoctrinated into the ways of the regular military.

The men received their arms on May 1. Uniforms shortly followed. Dressed in navy blue coats, navy flannel trousers and kepis with havelocks (for shading the necks of the men in the sunny South), the regiment was well equipped for war. On May 13, the newly trained soldiers left for Washington, D.C. Along the way, newspapers commented on the well-armed and finely uniformed men from Michigan.

On May 16 at 10:00 p.m., the First Regiment reached the city limits of the nation's capital. Abraham Lincoln heard the fuss of bands and citizens in the streets welcoming the troops. He asked what unit had arrived and, upon learning of the arrival of the Michiganders, is said to have exclaimed, "Thank God for Michigan!" The First Michigan became the first "western" regiment to reach Washington and eased Lincoln's concerns over the western states and their loyalty to the Federal government.[10]

Orlando Wilcox commanded the First Michigan. When asked by General Winfield Scott (commander of all Union forces) where the Michigan unit would like to make its camp, Wilcox pointed across the Potomac River to Arlington, Virginia. Eight days after arriving in the nation's capital, the First Michigan, along with Elmer Ellsworth's Fire Zouaves, marched into Arlington.

After taking control of Arlington, the First Michigan raised the Star-Spangled Banner over the marketplace. Ellsworth observed the Confederate flag waving over a local hotel, the Marshall House. The twenty-four-year-old colonel raced up to the hotel and ran inside to remove the flag. The rash action angered the owner, James T. Jackson, who shot Ellsworth dead. Jackson would later be bayoneted to death by a member of the Fire Zouaves. Colonel Wilcox assessed the situation and maintained the peace, preventing any retaliation against citizens of the town for the actions of one hotheaded individual.

Here, in enemy territory along the Potomac River, the First Michigan relaxed and awaited further action. The national holiday of July 4 would be celebrated by the members of the regiment: a morning dress parade was followed by John W. Horner (lieutenant in Company K and resident of Adrian) reciting the Declaration of Independence.[11]

The Second Michigan

In May, the Federal government ordered the states to make regiments "three-year" terms rather than the ninety-day terms for which many early volunteers had enlisted. This caused great confusion among the enlistees of the Second

Michigan. When faced with swearing an oath of service for three years rather than the shorter term, many men refused to serve. Several recruits from Adrian in Company D and from Hudson in Company B returned from Detroit upset over the change in mid-May. The regiment quickly filled the vacancies with men from the Detroit area seeking a company to enlist with.

On June 1, the *Hudson Gazette* brought the news of the death of a soldier to Lenawee County. John Canfield of Rollin had enlisted with the Lenawee Guards in Hudson in April. While drilling on the state fairgrounds, he took ill and was sent to the surgeon's tent. Other members of the regiment exhibited signs of illness, but Canfield's sickness worsened over the next few days. The twenty-eight-year-old died of congestive fever on May 28. His body was returned home to Rollin, where it was buried.

The regiment departed on June 6 for Washington, D.C. It took four days for the men to reach the nation's capital. Camp Winfield Scott became the home for men from Hudson and Adrian.

ADRIAN COLLEGE AND THE FOURTH REGIMENT

On May 16, Colonel Dwight Woodbury received official word that the Fourth Michigan Regiment would be accepted by the state for Federal service and that he should order the companies to a site of his choosing in Adrian for organization and drill. Woodbury opted to utilize the county fairgrounds, but due to a cold and wet spring, the grounds were flooded. Asa Mahan offered the use of the grounds at Adrian College for drill and for housing the regiment. The companies of the Fourth Michigan came from communities throughout southeast Michigan, including Adrian (Company B), Hudson (Company F) and Tecumseh (Company G).

The assembled men of the regiment adjusted to the routine of military life. A typical day began at 5:00 a.m. with reveille, breakfast at 6:30 a.m. and drill from 9:00 a.m. to 11:30 a.m., followed by a 12:30 p.m. midday meal. Drill resumed at 2:00 p.m. and ended with a dress parade at 5:00 p.m. Supper was at 6:30 p.m. in the dining hall of the college, and lights out occurred at 9:30 p.m.

The training camp was a source of entertainment for Adrian and surrounding communities. As many of the men were from Lenawee communities, several family members took the train into Adrian and would regularly watch the drills at what was dubbed "Camp Williams" (after Alpheus S. Williams, brigadier general of Michigan troops). A wagon ran

The Adrian College campus as it appeared in the 1860s. North Hall (building on the far right) housed the men of the Fourth Michigan Regiment. *Courtesy of Shipman Library, Adrian College.*

from the corner of Main and Maumee Streets, carrying passengers to Adrian College to see the excitement for ten cents round trip.

Soon, the novelty of one thousand men in town wore off on the citizens of Adrian. Fights among soldiers, public drunkenness and the comings and goings of the troops angered residents. Charles Cleveland reported a common occurrence for business owners: soldiers walking into businesses asking for cigars, tobacco and alcohol and, after receiving and consuming the items, ordering them to be charged to Uncle Sam.[12]

Uniforms and equipment started to arrive in early June. The men were clothed in gray coats and pants. Three hundred muskets, plus other arms scrounged up by Woodbury, meant only about half the regiment was armed by the time it was ready to head east to Washington.

On June 21, 1861, the men of the Fourth Regiment formed up in the afternoon for a special ceremony in which the unit would be presented with a regimental flag. Special trains brought onlookers from all corners of the state

Colonel Dwight D. Woodbury. *Courtesy of Lenawee County Historical Museum.*

of Michigan to see the unit one last time before it left the state. At 2:30 p.m., the Fourth formed a hollow square, and Mrs. Wilcox of Adrian presented the silk banner to Colonel Woodbury. Embroidered on the flag were the words: "The ladies of Adrian to the Fourth Regiment Michigan Infantry Defend It."

Woodbury received the flag and made a short speech. In part, he said:

> *In whatever position we may be assigned, with our banner to cheer us, we will strive to do our duty as American soldiers. To no inferior force shall it ever be surrendered, and sooner than be trailed to treason it shall become the pall of the regiment.*

The Fourth Michigan Regiment leaving Adrian. The men of the regiment marched up Maumee Street from Adrian College to the depot, where they boarded trains bound for Washington, D.C. *Courtesy of the Lenawee County Historical Society.*

As he closed his remarks, Woodbury told the ladies of Adrian that when the men followed the flag into battle, they would think of them.[13]

Three days after the ceremony, the Fourth Regiment boarded trains heading east.

OTHER UNITS VOLUNTEER

The number of men offering their services for the military far outstripped the number of spaces available in Lenawee County and across the state. The Federal government placed a quota system by state based on the population of the 1860 census. This meant that each state in the Union had to raise a certain percentage of troops based on the population of each congressional district.

As men agreed to serve under local military leaders, they found themselves left out of regiments formed within Michigan congressional districts. William Ward of Adrian raised a company of men, only to find out that there was no room for them. They offered up their services to the state of Ohio and were accepted into the Forty-seventh Ohio as Company B.

MANASSAS

Members of the First, Second and Fourth Michigan Regiments would find themselves in the grand move by Union general Irvin McDowell toward the Confederate capital of Richmond. At the railroad junction of Manassas, near the stream known as Bull Run, the first major battle of the Civil War occurred. The First and Second Michigan actively participated in the battle, while members of the Fourth Regiment observed from the fringes.

The Second Michigan reached a small ford along Bull Run known as Blackburn's Ford on the morning of July 18, 1861. The Union forces observed a strong body of Confederate troops under the command of General James Longstreet. An attempt by Federal forces (wanting to secure the river crossing) to drive the Rebels away failed, and a countercharge by Longstreet smashed into the Second Michigan troops. The regiment would be saved by the arrival of more Union forces under the command of William T. Sherman. The small skirmish at Blackburn's Ford set the stage for the main battle that occurred just three days later.

On July 21, the first major test of the young war arrived for both armies. The First Michigan fought in the afternoon near the Henry House and faced a Confederate leader who earned the nickname "Stonewall": General Thomas Jackson. Troops of the First Michigan, along with those from New York and Massachusetts, fought in a valiant attempt to retake a battery of Union artillery captured by Confederate forces. Under fire from both infantry and artillery, and sent into the field piecemeal and without support, the regiment soon ceased to be a fighting force. After the battle, reports stated that the First lost 150 men either killed, wounded or missing. One of the wounded men was Private Richard A. Watts. Watts recalled after the war riding back to Washington in an ambulance caked in his own blood from his wound while suffering from a case of the measles.[14]

DeGolyer Escape

While the Fourth Michigan was not directly involved in the Battle of Bull Run, some of the men of the regiment risked shot and shell to see the battle up close and personal. Captain Samuel DeGolyer of Hudson was one of the men who moved toward the sound of the battle. He found himself in a fluid situation. Union and Confederate forces had not standardized their uniforms, with Federal troops—including members of the Fourth Michigan—wearing gray. DeGolyer soon found himself amid enemy troops and was captured.

Members of the Fourth Regiment feared Captain DeGolyer and Lieutenant Simon Preston (of Hudson) had been killed. News reached Colonel Dwight Woodbury on August 11 that both DeGolyer and Preston were alive and being held prisoner in Richmond. The captives learned of rumors that they were soon to be moved to work on Rebel fortifications, possibly in North Carolina.

DeGolyer opted for a plan to escape. He approached Lieutenant Preston with this plan. Preston balked at the idea, but Quartermaster Sergeant Henry C. Jencks of the Second Rhode Island Infantry was willing to work with DeGolyer in any attempt to flee Rebel prison. (Preston would remain in Richmond for two months and then be transferred to Tuscaloosa, Alabama, for six months before being exchanged. He returned to the regiment in February 1862.)

On August 13, the pair went into action. They took advantage of the prison system, which allowed prisoners to cook their mess. Jencks and

Samuel DeGolyer from Hudson, Michigan, worked in a spoke factory prior to the outbreak of the Civil War. DeGolyer had a nose for a fight and often sought out danger during his service in the war. The *Hudson Gazette* wrote of him, "The fact is, Sam was spoiling for a fight and he wasn't born to be shot." *Courtesy of Hudson Museum.*

DeGolyer sought and received permission to go outside to the yard to cook. Somehow, the pair slipped away from the prison area. Jencks recounted:

> *On August 13 Capt DeGolyer and myself agreed on a plan of escape, which we carried into effect, but I would rather not tell how we effected it as it might injure others. We remained in a ravine for about 20 minutes when not hearing any alarm made at our escape, we judged that it was time to be off, and accordingly put out, exercising our ingenuity to avoid the sentinels which we did till we were about three miles out of Richmond, when we found ourselves in the midst of extensive fortifications. Thinking that soldiers were there we remained quiet for about three hours, when we again started and*

got safely through, having take our boots off and walking in our stockings to avoid making a noise. We had traveled about half a mile further when we came to a bridge without any planking. From the circumstance we judged that there were no soldiers in the neighborhood. We therefore crossed and traveled all night, but next morning we found, to our consternation that we had returned to the bridge. We then concealed ourselves in an extensive piece of woods, where we laid for about an hour, when some slaves made their appearance in the neighborhood and began to chop some large timbers for a fortification. We were much scared at this, and lay thinking how we should get out of the scrape, when the overseer made his appearance, and having hitched his horse to where the slaves were, when we crawled further into the wood, to a ditch covered over with briars. We procured some pieces of wood which we laid at the bottom of the ditch, on the mud, and lay on them the whole day. As soon as it was night we recommenced our journey and traveled about fifteen miles, having no other guide but the North star, which was not always visible, as it was very cloudy. The roads in that section of county are very intricate, and as we only traveled at night we often retraced our steps, towards the point we had started from. We had several hair-breath escapes, every day, seeing cavalry patrolling along the roads and compelling us to seek the shelter of the woods. On the 9th night we reached the bank of the Potomac, about ten miles from Aquia Creek and a little above Mathias Point. When we left Richmond we had ten cents worth of soda crackers and one loaf of white bread. By strict economy these lasted us five days. The rest of the time we subsisted on half an ear of raw green corn, and about a fill of raw wheat a piece. We had great trouble in crossing the other rivers till we came to the Potomac. On reaching that point it was just daybreak, when we ran nearly on a large body of cavalry, the horses of which were picketed near by. We fell back into the woods and lay there till night, when we went around the cavalry and struck the beach somewhat below. We walked up and down for three or four miles in search of a boat but could find none. We were, however, determined to make an attempt to cross for which purpose we picked up a quantity of driftwood and tying the pieces together with our clothing, made a raft. It was but a frail thing, but it was the best we could do under the circumstances. We started for the opposite shore, when to our consternation the raft began to go to pieces. I made up my mind that we would not be able to reach the shore. However we floated on for about half an hour more, when the raft struck against something and immediately went to pieces. Just then I felt a rope strike my face upon which Captain DeGolyer and myself reached upwards, caught the rope and

> *drew ourselves on to the deck of a vessel that was laden with tobacco; she proved to be the schooner* Catherine Jane *of Baltimore. The Captain and crew immediately rubbed us up, gave us warm drinks and wrapping us in blankets left us to our repose. We slept for about five hours, when we got up we felt quite refreshed. Shortly after, we were landed on the Maryland side, up which we walked for about ten miles when we came in sight of the blockading squadron of Aquia Creek. We hoisted a shirt on a pole as a signal, when a boat was lowered from the steamer Union, and took us on board, where we were treated with the greatest kindness, supplied with shoes and stockings and other necessaries and partook of a warm dinner of which we stood much in need. We then put on board the steam propeller* Josephine *of New York and taken to Washington DC where we arrived safely on August 23, 1861.*[15]

The pair were instant heroes, and the escape was national news. The men were sent to meet both General Winfield Scott and President Lincoln. After that, DeGolyer boarded a carriage to return him to the Fourth Regiment, where the men cheered the return of their comrade. DeGolyer was given a pass to return to Hudson in early September to recoup and recruit.

DeGolyer canvassed Lenawee County seeking recruits and had successfully enlisted nearly one hundred men by the end of September. One of the men recruited was Albert H. Boies of Hudson, who had just turned seventeen and was a member of the Hudson Zouave Cadets. His parents signed off on the enlistment with the condition that Albert was not to serve in the ranks.

DeGolyer rented a building at the corner of Main and High Streets in Hudson from a Mr. Gillett and Niles for the sum of thirty cents per man per day. Locally, the building became known as "Camp DeGolyer."

Governor Austin Blair promoted DeGolyer to the rank of major. The promotion filled a vacancy in the Fourth Michigan created when Lieutenant Colonel William Duffield left to become commander of the Ninth Michigan. This "meddling" of the governor angered Colonel Woodbury, for DeGolyer snuck off to see the battle at Bull Run rather than remaining with the rest of the regiment. In December 1861, DeGolyer faced trumped-up charges for ordering his men to obtain doors and windows from a home belonging to a Southern family. Facing a court-martial trial, DeGolyer resigned his post on January 13, 1862, and began seeking a new role in the war.

First Michigan Returns

The term of enlistment for the First Michigan ended on August 7, 1861, as the men had enlisted for three-month terms. The men were brought back to Detroit, paid for their service and mustered out. When Company K returned to Adrian, Charles Croswell, now mayor of Adrian, welcomed them back to town.

Several of the men would reenlist in the coming months. Many joined the Seventeenth Michigan in the spring of 1862. Two men from the First returned to their school; Jerome Fee and Richard Watts both enrolled in the fall term at Adrian College. In June 1862, both men rejoined the war effort.

Recruitment Continues

After the defeat of the Union forces at Bull Run, the view of a short war came to a close. Both sides were well aware that the other forces would indeed fight. Several politicians became concerned that recruits would no longer volunteer for dangerous duty. The support of the Union was never stronger in Michigan and Lenawee County. Reports of captured troops at Manassas were one reason there were many volunteers stepping forward to take their place. The many enlistees in the Berdan Sharpshooters and the Eleventh Michigan are prime examples of patriotic spirit and civic duty remaining strong in Lenawee.

The Berdan Sharpshooters were an elite military unit formed by Hiram Berdan. Berdan was a mechanical engineer who had an interest in competitive shooting prior to the Civil War. At the outbreak of the war, he recruited eighteen companies of expert marksmen to serve the Union.

Any potential recruit for his unit had to pass a shooting contest to gain the right to enlist in the regiment. Interested parties shot ten times at a target two hundred yards away. After each shot, the judge took a measurement from the center of the target to the entry hole of the bullet. The measurements were then added; only those with a score of less than fifty were qualified to enlist.

The contest in Hudson took place in late July. The *Hudson Gazette* reported that eighteen applicants were accepted, including notable Hudson names like Simeon Van Akin, Jason Schermerhorn and Henry Ten Eyck, to name a few. In October, judges returned to Hudson to offer the test again. Franklin

Franklin Cobb was one of nearly fifty marksmen from Lenawee County who joined the elite sharpshooters. Cobb penned letters back to the *Hudson Gazette* updating the community on the members of Company C, the Michigan-based company of the First United States Sharpshooters. *Courtesy of Hudson Museum.*

Cobb, William and Calvin Colwell and John Wirts joined the others from the Hudson area.

Newspaper reports talked about the formation of a company of infantry gathering in Hudson in August. Called Colonel May's Independent Regiment, enlistees from Morenci, Hudson, Medina and other areas of southwestern Lenawee County joined the unit at Hudson. By September, the State of Michigan had accepted the unit, and it became known as the Eleventh Michigan Infantry. The Hudson group was designated as Company F.

Camp Baker was the drill ground for the men of Company F. Located on the farm of state senator William Baker on West Street, the men used the barn as a barracks and the pastureland for maneuvers. Local ladies visited daily to deliver cakes and pies to the men. By September 14, the call had come for Company F to rendezvous with the rest of the regiment in White Pigeon, Michigan. Before the men left, Reverend L. Smith Hobart of the Hudson Congregational Church was appointed chaplain of the Eleventh.

Opposing Viewpoint

While the disaster at Bull Run redoubled the war effort on the homefront in Lenawee County, the mood on the front lines was not as optimistic. Dr. David Chamberlain of Hudson joined the Michigan as the assistant regimental surgeon. He penned a series of letters to the *Hudson Gazette* describing the sights the members, especially the members from Hudson, of the Fourth came across on their war efforts.

After the Battle of Bull Run, Chamberlain offered his assessment of the war in a letter dated July 24 (published in the *Hudson Gazette* on August 3):

> *We have underrated our enemy very much; the kind of balls and shells fired into our camps, demonstrated that they had an abundance of the most improved and valuable patterns. . . . The whole people seem to be engaged in the business heart and soul. . . . These people are fighting as they firmly believe, to protect their hearthstones, their wives and children, and their property, from the ruthless hand of a hireling soldiery. Can we convince them of their error?*

In another letter dated July 31 that would be published in the August 10 edition of the *Hudson Gazette*, Chamberlain noted a loss of patriotism in the ranks as he waded through numerous applications for medical discharges. He offered the following in closing:

> *There is a great deal of anxiety on the part of officers, about a certain examination which is to come off, and old Hardee's Tactics are seen in all the camps. That is a move in the right direction. It was demonstrated at the Battle of Bull Run that the fault was not in the men, but the officers. . . . It was found to be bad policy to learn them military tactics*

in the teeth of batteries . . . so the order has been issued to examine all officers, and such as cannot show sufficient knowledge are to be sent home.

The two letters caused great concern back on the homefront, and many questioned Dr. Chamberlain's commitment to the cause. He would continue to author letters vividly recounting events with the regiment, but rather than sign his name, he opted for the penname "The Recruit."

3

1862: The Year of Jubilee

The dawn of the new year brought many challenges to citizens of Lenawee County. What people once thought would be a short war now looked to be a lengthy endeavor. Men in Lenawee continued to enlist in new regiments that sprang to life during the year. By December 1862, men from the area were serving throughout the South in fields near Shiloh, Richmond, Antietam Creek and Fredericksburg. The goal of the war would change as well. When the war started, Northern troops fought to keep the nation whole. Now the war was being fought to end slavery, thanks to help from a resident of Lenawee serving in Congress.

Fifteenth Michigan and Shiloh

The Fifteenth Michigan began the process of enlisting troops in late 1861, but the unit would not gain full strength until March 1862. The core of the unit would be made up of three-month enlistees who, upon returning home in August 1861, worked to find a way back to the front. David Clark of Deerfield provides an example of the early enlistees in the Fifteenth Michigan.

Clark was eighteen years old when Confederate forces fired on Fort Sumter. Private Clark enlisted in Company K of the First Michigan Infantry and served for three months. His discharge came on August 7, 1861. Seeking a chance to serve again, Clark joined the Fifteenth on December 28, 1861. Thanks to his prior military service, Clark became sergeant of Company H.

The unit rendezvoused on the grounds of the Monroe Fairgrounds and Agricultural Association. The men drilled on the grounds and slept in a repurposed large frame building that acted as a makeshift barracks. On March 20, 1862, the men were formally mustered into service. The members of the regiment included over one hundred soldiers from Lenawee.

The unit left Monroe on March 27, 1862, and arrived at Pittsburg Landing, Tennessee, on April 5, 1862. They camped near the riverboat landing and would be attached to General Benjamin Prentiss's command. At dawn, the men of the Fifteenth reported hearing the popping of rifle fire in the woods to their front. When officers reported the gunfire up the chain of command, the reply was that it must be hunters, as there were no Confederate forces within miles of the Union camp.

The only Federal officer who was leery of Confederates in the front was Colonel William Graves. Graves, from Adrian, had been wounded in action at Bull Run while serving with the First Michigan. Now with the Twelfth Michigan and under Prentiss, Graves sent out pickets, who reported numerous enemy campfires. Graves left pickets out overnight.

What the Union pickets from Prentiss's division found were the lead elements of a Confederate attack. When wounded Federal troops began streaming back from the woods, the men of the Fifteenth Michigan formed up into a battle line and marched toward the sound of the fight.

Finding Prentiss and other Federal regiments engaged with the enemy, the Fifteenth fell in on the left of the Sixty-first Illinois along a ridge. Soon, a large body of Confederate troops gathered on the opposing ridge. As a new unit on the field, the raw troops of the Fifteenth Michigan prepared for the Confederate advance.

As the enemy forces fired into the men from southeastern Michigan, no fire was returned. The men stood fast at order arms, as the Fifteenth Michigan had not yet been supplied with ammunition. Men began to fall, killed and wounded. Officers realized the catastrophic nature of the situation, and the Fifteenth Michigan hastily retreated to the rear.

George McBride, from Deerfield, in Company H recalled his take on the situation for the green troops:

> *The enemy flank us and are moving to our rear; some one* [sic] *calls out "Everybody for himself!" The line breaks, I go with others, back and down the hill, across a small ravine, and into the camp of the 11th Illinois cavalry*

> *with the howling, rushing mass of the enemy pressing in close pursuit. . . . The striking of shot on the ground threw up little clouds of dust, and the falling of men all around me impressed me with a desire to get out of there. . . . I felt sure that a cannon-ball was close behind me, giving me chase as I started for the river. . . . I never ran so fast before.*[16]

The episode of the Fifteenth Michigan was a microcosm of how the day went for the Federal forces at Shiloh. Confederates swept the field on April 6. General Ulysses Grant spent the evening planning for a counterattack. The day of April 7 found members of the Fifteenth Michigan, this time with ammunition, fighting with men from General Alexander McCook's division. In his after-action report, McCook wrote that the Fifteenth was "under the hottest fire," and the men "acted with conspicuous gallantry."[17]

The Fifteenth Michigan had ninety-six men killed, wounded or missing in the two days of fighting at what became known as the Battle of Shiloh. News reports filtered home of the local men killed and wounded in action, including Robert Craig of Palmyra. While the Union forces did win the battle, it was at a cost of over twenty-three thousand killed, wounded or missing on both sides.

The Fifteenth Michigan and the Union armies in Tennessee followed the Confederate forces to Corinth, Mississippi, and laid siege to the city, an operation that lasted until the end of May.

Battery H, First Michigan Light Artillery

While men trained in the Fifteenth Michigan Infantry at Monroe, there was another unit being raised at the same place and time. A battery of artillery had been attached to the Fifteenth Michigan, and the officers worked toward filling the ranks. Nearly thirty men from Lenawee County served in the ranks of what would come to be known by the monikers of "DeGolyer's Battery" or "Eighth Michigan Black Horse Artillery."

The leader of the battery would be Samuel DeGolyer. After resigning from the Fourth Michigan, DeGolyer returned to Michigan to seek appointment in a regiment. His time spent escaping imprisonment in the South and relying on assistance from slaves turned DeGolyer from a Democrat fighting to preserve the Union into a newly minted Republican fighting to end slavery.

As such, the Republican administration in Lansing worked to find a way to work a war hero and supporter into a leading role.

That opportunity came with the battery attached to the Fifteenth Michigan. On March 9, 1862, the *Hudson Gazette* reported that Samuel DeGolyer would be captain of the battery in Monroe. Thanks to reports of incompetency in the leadership of the battery, the State of Michigan removed the previous captain (M.L. Lockwood).

DeGolyer had little time to get to know the officers and men of his new assignment, as the battery was ordered to report to St. Louis to begin operations against the Confederate position at Island Number 10. In a letter to the *Hudson Gazette* published on April 25, Captain DeGolyer described the work the men of the battery were performing against the Confederates:

> *We have batteries at short distances all along the river so that if the rebels undertake to run their boats up to relieve their friends at Island No 10 or to come down with those up there to join their friends below they will stand a better chance of going to the bottom than joining their friends. Every day one of their gunboats comes down to reconnoiter but is careful to keep just beyond the range of our guns. The rebels are busy on the other side of the river throwing up earthworks. They work all night and as soon it is light we open fire on them and they scatter. Night before last we ranged our guns upon an unfinished earthwork built the night previous, getting the range and distance before dark. We lay perfectly quiet until about 10 o'clock when we could hear them at work again, and then let go two of our 32 pounders, charged with shot and shell, both of which exploded just at the point intended. Such a scattering up and down. Although when we fired all was darkness over there lights were immediately seen flying around. In the morning one of our boys hollered to two or three that could be seen "You had a good time over there last night." "Yes damn you, you shot too low."*

The long siege for control of the Mississippi River by DeGolyer's Battery ended on April 8. After the siege was over, the members of the battery spent time drilling, equipping the unit and breaking in horses. The extended time spent near Island Number 10 made it possible for Mrs. DeGolyer to join her husband. In August, she made the trip and wrote the following about her journey and the exploits of DeGolyer, which would be published in the *Hudson Gazette* on September 6:

When within 15 miles of Island No 10 on Sunday night the steamer was fired into by guerrillas, injuring no one, but frightening the women and children. The Captain requested the boat to stop at Island No 10 where he procured a number of cavalrymen and brought them to New Madrid and taking a number of his own men, making about 70 in all, started off in pursuit of them across the county. They traveled from 6 Monday morning until 8 in the evening being 14 hours in the saddle without dismounting or feeding, when they took them by surprise killing four, wounding many and taking three captains and 15 privates prisoners. His loss was one horse killed. He took 23 horses, 100 guns, saddles etc. I had the pleasure of seeing the prisoners at the landing when that Captain took them on the Rob Roy, *a government boat to General Quinby at Columbus, where they will be tried by a military commission and probably some will be sentenced to be shot during the week. I think the Captain would have gone again last night, had he been here, as a Union resident came into camp shortly after his departure to inform him where there is another encampment. I wish you could have been here when the boys returned with their prisoners, who were very bad men, particularly one of the captains. The camp here is pleasantly located on the river bank, above the fortifications. Our tent is under a large oak tree with a matched planed floor 12 x 35 feet in front covered by the tree, under which seats are arranged for the battery boys to rest themselves and where the colored individuals sometimes amuse the boys with their pranks.*

War in the East: "On to Richmond"

Members of the Second and Fourth Michigan in the Army of the Potomac followed General George McClellan in his spring offensive against Richmond. The Federal troops moved out on March 17, and by early May, elements of the Union army found themselves facing off with Confederate forces around Revolutionary War sites in Virginia like Yorktown and Williamsburg. Slowly, McClellan maneuvered his forces toward the Confederate capital of Richmond.

The Second Michigan participated in the fighting around Yorktown and Williamsburg. T.C. Barden of Hudson recounted the movements in a May 25 letter published in the *Hudson Gazette*:

You have doubtless been informed by telegraph that the rebels left Yorktown on Saturday night last and on Sunday morning early the pursuit began. We

> *followed closely on this regiment however following as rear guard. Sunday night we bivouacked about a mile this side of Yorktown. Yesterday morning Berry's brigade the 2nd, 3rd, and 5th Michigan and 37 New York regiment were ordered to the front to sustain the Division that was attacking the rebels line of entrenchments a mile to the front of Williamsburg. The rain was falling in torrents, the roads cut up so as to be almost impassable by the passage of wagons and artillery, mud so deep that often the troops sank in up to their knees but we pushed on for about ten miles, getting in position about 2 pm. We were immediately pushed to the front to relieve the troops that had been engaged all day. Company B was ordered as skirmishers, into an abbatis of falled trees in front of the enemy's rifle pits and fortifications. With heroic valor the men went in. The regiment soon after went in on the left of our Company. Until dark we kept the enemy at bay, and drove them out of the abbatis, even. It was a terrible place, exposed as we were to the cross fires of several regiments of rebel infantry besides artillery.*

The Fourth Michigan would see its first battle while maneuvering toward Richmond. At a river crossing along the Chickahominy River, at a place known as New Bridge, a young cavalry officer by the name of George Armstrong Custer led the Fourth Michigan against the Fifth Louisiana. The officers and men of the Fourth were well acquainted with Custer, as he had lived in Monroe prior to the war. Custer was under orders to probe the strength of the enemy at New Bridge, and the Fourth Regiment was the first infantry that he came across on his search for reinforcements.

The fight lasted around four hours from start to finish, and the Fourth drove the enemy from the field. Forced to ford a swollen river, the men of the Fourth waded, swam and willed their way toward the enemy. The enemy had fifty killed and wounded; fifty more were taken prisoner. Only two men from the Fourth were killed in the action: Able Piper and Franklin Drake, both from Lenawee.

Colonel Woodbury received accolades from General McClellan for his successful command of his troops in the face of the enemy. McClellan said, "Colonel, I am happy to congratulate you again on your success." Turning to the men of the Fourth, he asked, "Do you think anything can stop you from going to Richmond?" The men cried out "No!" with great enthusiasm.[18]

Dr. Chamberlain of the Fourth Michigan gave an idea of the kind of land the men from Lenawee County were fighting in. Published in the May 31 edition of the *Hudson Gazette*, the letter in part said:

> *Just imagine a line of men strung along from your town* [Hudson] *to Clayton village and over a much rougher country, interspersed with small streams and swampy, boggy land. Then further imagine the enemy's line of fortifications on the south line of the townships, say three miles away. Now this whole space of territory three miles wide and six miles long, to have at least three distinct ditches for trenches, say five feet deep by six to eight feet wide, running the whole distance, making it in one line a ditch as far from Hudson to Adrian.*

He went on to describe the fortifications made for the artillery, gabbons (baskets made of branches and filled with dirt to protect men and entrenchments from artillery) and the enemy landmines (known then as torpedoes). Modern war had arrived, yet the tactics of the war were from the past.

On May 31, Joseph Johnson's Confederate forces attempted to destroy a portion of Union forces isolated by the flooded Chickahominy River. The Second Michigan assisted in stemming the Rebel attack by charging into the advancing enemy. Edward Barkway and George Jenkins, both of Hudson, fell wounded in the fight. Jenkins would be discharged from the army for his wounds. Barkway was less fortunate, as a comrade reported:

> *Edwin Barkway of Hudson fell wounded, several of our men passed him, but the rebels were pressing our front and both flanks and they thought they could not bear him off; his wounds were not mortal and we hoped the fortune of the day would soon enable us to get him again, or at worst we would hear of him as a wounded prisoner. But alas, the spirit of succession* [sic] *has made fiends of the Southern soldiers, and Sunday night we found him, but he had been murdered! As he lay wounded in the woods where he fell, some cowardly rebel had put his gun to poor Barkway's forehead and blown out his brains. The powder was blown into his face, showing clearly that he had been killed by none other than the murderer's hand. Poor Ed! He was the life of the company.*[19]

On June 26, the new commander of the Confederate Army of Northern Virginia lashed out at the Union forces near Richmond. Robert E. Lee ordered troops to attack near a bend in the Chickahominy River known as Beaver Dam Creek, near Mechanicsville. Elements of the Fourth Michigan were ordered to move toward the sound of battle in light marching order.

The fight was well underway by the time the Fourth Michigan arrived on the field in the late afternoon, just as a group of Pennsylvania troops were

Unknown company of the Second Michigan Infantry. *Courtesy of Bentley Historical Library.*

running out of ammunition. The Fourth received orders to come onto line on the far right. Here, the regiment became engaged with Rebel forces in a sharp but short firefight in a tangle of woods and brush. Driving the enemy from the field, the Union forces were victorious.

After the fight, Dr. Chamberlain reported "about twenty killed, wounded and missing." In after-action reports, Lieutenant George Monteith of Adrian received accolades for his actions in carrying orders, directing reinforcements and rallying the troops. Monteith had been a schoolteacher prior to the war and enlisted in Company G of the Fourth Michigan. During the battle, he was serving as an aide to General Fitz John Porter and would later gain an appointment to make that a permanent position in September 1862.

Overnight, McClellan ordered the Union Fifth Corps, including the Fourth Michigan, to fall back to a defensive position near Gaines Mill. This maneuver meant that the regiment would be acting as a rear guard for the entire army. Chamberlain wrote, "Our route led us through our old camp. . . . We found our hospital tents still standing, filled with the sick, and everything as we had left it, the rebels only two miles in our rear." The doctor hastily selected a few items to take with him on the march and then burned the rest, lest it fall in Rebel hands.[20]

By 9:00 a.m., on June 27, the Fourth Michigan found itself in position along the crest of a hill on farmland near Boatsawin's Swamp. The regiment held the center of the First Division's line on the left of the Fifth Corps' line. Here the men rested after spending time building breastworks to defend any attack.

At three o'clock in the afternoon, the sound of gunfire brought the men to attention. Given the task to delay oncoming Confederate forces, the Fourth easily brushed off three disjointed probing attacks. Rebel troops emerging from the woods were hit by rifle fire and faced being shot to pieces if they continued across the open fields.

In the late afternoon, Confederate general John Bell Hood's Texas brigade poured out of the woods, charging across the open field and up the hill toward the Union lines. The timing of the attack was nearly perfect; the ferocity of the attack, combined with a gap created by one Union regiment being replaced by fresh troops, placed the men of the Fourth in a bad position. Soon, the members of the regiment were taking gunfire from the the front and side while running low on munitions.

The men of the Fourth fell back in an orderly fashion to the rear, where there were reserves. Colonel Woodbury, determined to fight the Confederates for every inch of ground, planted the regimental colors in an open field and ordered the soldiers to rally. The officers and men, seeing the act of bravery and defiance, streamed out from the woods and toward the colonel to form a battle line.

The situation quickly deteriorated for the regiment. Federal forces on the right and left of the Michiganders fell back, exposing the Fourth to a murderous crossfire. Compelled to retire, the men made for the rear as best they could. George Millens of Medina wrote after the battle, "We retreated about one mile & met some reinforcements & halted & formed. . . . We were soon supplied with ammunition & were ready to go in but were not needed."[21]

The fight at Gaines Mill cost the Fourth over eighty men killed, wounded and missing. The killed included Simon B. Preston of Hudson and Jeptha Beers of Tecumseh (who died of wounds on July 6). The survivors of the action slept on the ground without bedrolls and blankets, as their knapsacks had been burned to keep them from Confederate hands.

By noon on June 28, 1862, the survivors of the Fourth Michigan were on the move again. General McClellan had had enough of the attempt to take Richmond and maneuvered his troops back to the safety of the James

River. Here, the Federal troops could receive supplies and board ships to retreat back to Washington, D.C. The march measured thirteen miles as the arrow flies but would be longer, as the winding roads and swollen rivers of Virginia meant the men had to take a meandering path.

For three days, the troops in the Fourth Michigan made their way to the safety of the James River. On the afternoon of June 30, Union forces—including the Fourth—gathered on and around a strong defensive position on a tall hill and the surrounding ridges known as Malvern Hill.

On the morning of July 1, the Fourth Michigan received the order to move out in front of Malvern Hill to support the artillery battery on top of the position. Lee's troops struck to the right of the men in a probing attack to determine the strength of the Federal position. In the early afternoon, Rebels appeared in front of the Michigan men but did not push an attack. Soon, a lull developed in the afternoon heat of the South.

In the early evening, the silence broke. Confederate artillery opened on the battery above the regiment. The cannonade lasted nearly half an hour, and then came the Southern troops, pouring out of the woods directly in front of the Fourth. Dr. Chamberlain recalled that the "whizzing, whirring and whistling of every species of projectile was perfectly bewildering. . . . Still that mass of human beings came rushing on."[22]

The enemy closed to within one hundred yards before Woodbury's troops opened fire. Volley after volley poured into the Confederates, yet on they came with fresh troops. The fierce fighting went on for half an hour before the regiment next to the Fourth Michigan charged after a group of fleeing Confederate troops. The men of the Ninth Massachusetts soon entered into the path of the rifles of the Fourth Michigan.

Officers of the Fourth ordered their men to cease fire as fellow troops chased in close pursuit of the Rebels. The charge was brief, as the Rebels reorganized and now charged the Federal position without gunfire to check their advance. Woodbury rushed to the fleeing soldiers of the Ninth, imploring them to re-form the ranks to check the oncoming enemy.

An officer rallying troops becomes a target for riflemen, and in this moment, Colonel Woodbury was killed. Struck in the head, Woodbury died instantly.[23] Woodbury's corpse would be carried off the field and into the woods. While this went on, the other officers of the Fourth Michigan worked quickly to clear the Ninth Massachusetts out of the way.

With the friendly forces out of the line of fire and the enemy pressing in, the soldiers of the Fourth Michigan "went at it tooth and nail," Marshall

The diary of Albert Boies saved his life when he was shot at Malvern Hill. Boies was knocked head over heels when the round struck him, and he recounted that it felt like he had been hit with a sledgehammer. *Courtesy of Amanda Ebbutt.*

Chapin, captain of Company F, recalled.[24] In the desperate struggle, the men fired as many as eighty rounds, and ammunition became scarce. Running out of ammunition, energy and daylight, the men of the Fourth would fall back under the protective cover of U.S. Sharpshooters and the battery atop Malvern Hill.

The battle cost the Fourth Michigan its commander and fifty-three others killed in action. Jonathan Childs replaced Woodbury as commander. The men spent most of July recouping from illnesses contracted from the swamps, fatigue and battles of the last few weeks and would not move from James River until after August 10. The Fourth Michigan boarded ferries to make its way back to the Manassas Junction area and then acted as a rear guard as the Union army retreated once again from Bull Run.

The Union forces near Richmond retreated to Washington, D.C. The pullback allowed Lee and the Confederates to move north. The two forces met at Manassas. Soldiers from Lenawee County served in units that provided support to the engaged forces during the battle.

Company C of the First United States Sharpshooters did see action at Second Manassas. Company C was primarily men from Michigan and included over twenty men from the Hudson area. Franklin Cobb (Hudson) penned a letter to the *Hudson Gazette* (published on September 6) recounting the action at Bull Run:

> *Shell, shot, bullets, etc. flew faster than I have every heard them before. Our regiment got together about dark and that night retreated to Centerville. There was hardly a man in Company C who was not hit by something. A small piece of shell hit my rubber blanket, which was thrown over my shoulders. William Cowell (of Hudson) was hit several times, so was Almeron "Cal" Armstrong.*

RECRUITING OFFICES OPEN—AGAIN

The severe losses to the the Union armies at Shiloh, outside Richmond, and at Bull Run led to a shortage of manpower. Lincoln called for more manpower to end the war—another 300,000 men in July. Such a call led to the formation of the Seventeenth and Eighteenth Michigan during the late summer of 1862.

The members of the Seventeenth Michigan, Company A, were primarily from Adrian and the surrounding countryside. Some of the recruits—such as Richard A. Watts, who became a second lieutenant in the unit—had served in the ninety-day First Michigan. Under the command of Loren Comstock, the unit gathered in Detroit with the other companies in August.

The Eighteenth Michigan's members mainly came from Lenawee and Hillsdale Counties, although they did take in recruits from Monroe. Companies A, B, C, E and I came from Lenawee County. The companies gathered in Hillsdale to train for the war. By September, the Eighteenth Michigan was on its way to Tennessee.

Besides the men enlisting in infantry regiments, several men from Lenawee enlisted in cavalry regiments. Elliott Gray of Tecumseh became lieutenant of Company B in the Seventh Michigan Cavalry. Several men from around Adrian became part of Company F of the Fourth Michigan Cavalry.

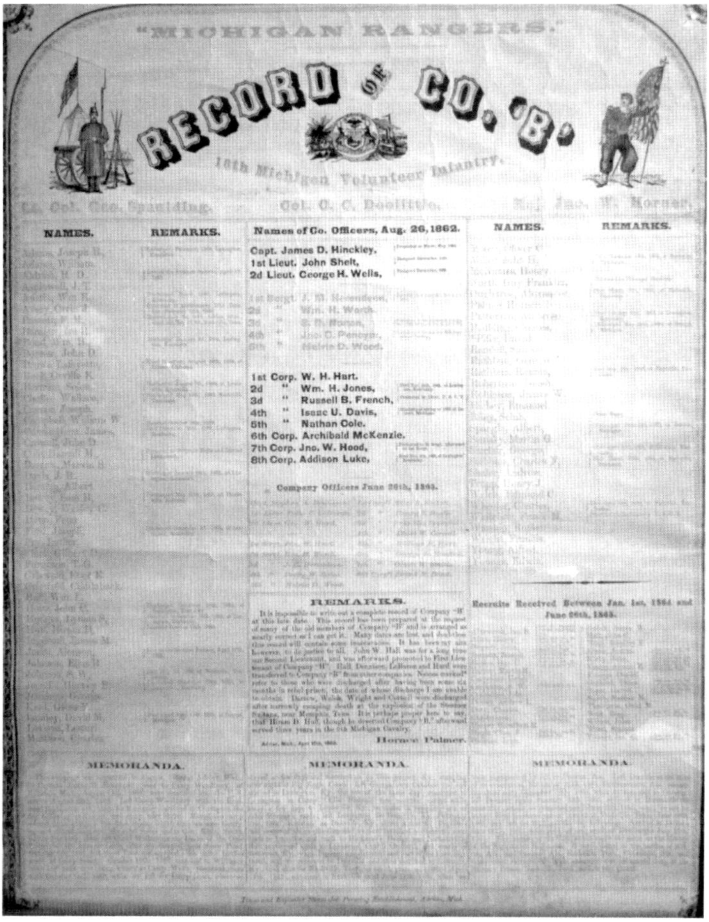

A poster listing the roster of Company B of the Eighteenth Michigan Infantry. *Courtesy of Lenawee County Historical Museum.*

Antietam Campaign

Antietam was the single bloodiest day of the Civil War. Over twenty-three thousand men were killed or wounded in the one-day fight on September 17. Men from Lenawee County played limited roles during that day but were active in the events leading up to the battle and in the events after the fight.

For the Seventeenth Michigan, the Antietam campaign would be its first foray into fighting. The regiment arrived in Washington, D.C., in early September. The unit was assigned to the Ninth Corps when Lee advanced into Maryland.

On September 14, the Seventeenth Michigan found itself in Middleton, near South Mountain. George B. McClellan, the commander of the Union Army of the Potomac, had in his possession Lee's plan for the Maryland Campaign. Known as "Lee's Lost Order," or "Special Order #191," the Confederate army was split into three smaller groups, with only a few regiments guarding the gaps of South Mountain.

The Ninth Corps moved forward to attack Turner's and Fox's Gaps. At the crest of South Mountain, near Fox's Gap, the Seventeenth met Confederates in a defensive position along a stone wall. The Seventeenth charged the position and drove the enemy from the field, earning the nickname the "Stonewall Regiment." The green troops acted like veterans and, after the battle, reported 27 killed and 114 wounded.

At the Battle of Antietam on September 17, the Seventeenth Michigan participated in the charge up from Antietam Creek toward Sharpsburg after Union forces gained control of the lower bridge (known now as Burnside's Bridge). Here, the men stormed up from the waterway toward the plateau

A famous photo of President Lincoln and General McClellan after the Battle of Antietam. Captain George Monteith (of Adrian) with the Fourth Michigan stands second from the left in Alexander Gardner's photo. Monteith was an aide for General Porter. *Courtesy of the Library of Congress.*

and the awaiting Rebels. The short fight cost the regiment another eighteen killed and eighty-seven wounded.

The Fourth Michigan engaged the retreating Confederate forces at Shepardstown, Virginia (now West Virginia), on September 19. Surging across the Potomac River, the Fourth Michigan set its sights on an abandoned battery of artillery on the bank of the river. Met with fire when the unit came out of the woods onto the opposite bank, the Fourth Michigan would be joined by the First U.S. Sharpshooters.

The men forded the river and, with a shriek, charged at the hidden Rebels. Seeing a superior force, the Confederates abandoned the guns. Silas Sadler of Tecumseh in Company G wrote, "Whenever there is a river to cross they always seem to call on our regiment." He added, "When we left Michigan we had eleven hundred and forty men now we have only got 300 . . . that is using them up pretty fast."[25]

Politics after Antietam

After the Union victory at Antietam, Abraham Lincoln issued a preliminary Emancipation Proclamation. The order freed all slaves in territories not in Federal command. Lincoln stated that the official war act would go into effect on January 1, 1863. The war was now about slavery and preservation of the Union.

The proclamation ending slavery was not a new step in the political arena. Fernando Beaman and other members of Congress had worked over the summer months to find ways to do so. On July 17, President Lincoln signed into law the Second Confiscation Act, which directly freed slaves in Union lines that were engaged in any rebellion or insurrection.

Beaman fully supported the legislation. He wrote that "his Government has been wickedly assaulted and besieged by traitors." He went on to say, "The original and continuing cause of the rebellion is slavery, and all attempts to conceal or disguise the fact are simply absurd." Emancipation was critical to the war effort, Beaman argued. "I am in favor of liberating the slaves of the rebels."[26]

FREDERICKSBURG

George B. McClellan would be removed again from command of the Army of the Potomac. Members of the Second and Fourth Michigan found themselves under the command of Ambrose Burnside. Rather than go into winter encampment, he opted to try to fight the Confederates. The army moved south to engage the enemy. Dr. Chamberlain wrote in a letter published in the *Hudson Gazette* on December 13:

> *We have been on the march and the weather is so cold that my fingers could not hold a pen. Now we have camped and I have got an old bake kettle full of coals in my tent so I can keep them warm. When last I wrote you we were stopping near Sharpsburg, MD. After a long unaccountable delay we started across the Potomac at Harper's Ferry and made our way down the east side of the Blue Ridge, passing through Loudon County in Virginia.*

At one o' clock in the afternoon on December 13, the Fourth Michigan crossed the Rappahannock River into the town of Fredericksburg. The men hunkered down and waited for the order to advance. At 3:00 p.m., the Fourth's portion of the attack took place.

The Fourth charged toward the Confederate works on top of Marye's Heights. Pressing into the ground to hide from Rebel shot and shell, the men rose only to fire at the enemy. Only fourteen men in the regiment would die, and forty-one were wounded—a low number considering the casualties of other units in this battle. The Fourth was one of the last Federal units into the fray, and as such, darkness ended the battle for the day. The men of the Fourth were not given the order to withdraw after the fighting, forcing the men to lay in the field among the dead and wounded.

The next day, men of the Fourth assumed the battle would commence at dawn. Both sides waited for the other to make a move. George Millens of Medina recalled, "We are still upon the front skirmishing. . . . We lay flat on our faces." In the prone position, the men of the Fourth were able to avoid Confederate sharpshooters who would fire on anything that moved.[27] When night came, the men got the order to retire from the field and slowly backed down the hill into town—and the fight was over.

Adrian College would feel the long-term sting of the actions at Fredericksburg. In 1861, Theodore Mahan, son of President Asa Mahan, joined the Sixteenth Michigan Infantry as the first lieutenant in Company

D. By August 1862, Mahan had received a promotion to become the captain of Company D.

At Fredericksburg, the Sixteenth Michigan attacked Marye's Heights. The regiment crossed the Rappahannock River at 4:30 p.m. and attacked at 6:20 p.m. The attack came after sunset, with only flashes of rifle and cannon fire to guide the troops to their target atop the hill. The attack failed, and in the process the unit lost nearly two hundred men, killed or wounded.

One of the wounded men was Theodore Mahan. Mahan spent time in the Union hospitals in Virginia. His mother, Mary, left Adrian to be by his side and help nurse him back to health. Eventually, Mahan was moved back to the Cleveland, Ohio area, but his health took a turn for the worse. Theodore Mahan died on June 23, 1863, due to his wounds from the battle.

The death of his only son deeply affected Asa Mahan. Mahan wrote letters critical of the war effort to Abraham Lincoln and other members of the government. After the war, he authored a book examining the tactics used during the conflict.

4

1863: Lenawee on Two Fronts

At the start of the new year, men from Lenawee found themselves battling in southern Tennessee, near Murfreesboro, in what was known as the Battle of Stones River. The Eleventh Michigan was a relatively green unit in the western theater. It spent the year 1862 in garrison and on guard duty in and around Nashville, Tennessee. On December 31, 1862, Stones River would be the first major conflict for the troops.

Confederate general Braxton Bragg, seeking to dislodge Union forces under General Phil Sheridan and splinter the line, spent the afternoon directing a series of assaults on a salient force that had formed in the Round Forest, known after the battle as "Hell's Half-Acre." The Eleventh Michigan held the apex of the line, which bent back on either side of the unit. Here, men from Lenawee County slugged it out with Rebel forces. Colonel Stoughton of the Eleventh recalled, "The fire of the enemy was apparently concentrated on this point and it was terrific. . . . The slaughter was great and men and officers fell on every side."[28]

When Federal units to the right of the Eleventh began to run out of ammunition, they fell back and retreated. This caused the Eleventh Michigan to retreat from its position as well. The untested unit acted like veterans, retreating a few yards and then turning around to fire a volley to check Confederate advances.

January 1, 1863, passed while both armies reorganized and drew up battle plans. On the afternoon of January 2, Confederate forces renewed their attack. The Eleventh Michigan provided support to a mass of artillery that would be attacked by Confederate general John C. Breckinridge. When the Rebel troops came into view, the batteries opened fire, along with a horrific volley from the Federal infantry. The withering fire checked the Confederate advance, and further volleys forced the enemy to retreat. The Eleventh Michigan let out a cheer—the battle was over, and it had performed well in its first real test at a cost of thirty-two dead, ninety-nine wounded and twenty-nine missing.

Lenawee County troops in the Eleventh suffered in the Battle of Stones River. Eighteen men would be among the rolls of killed, wounded or missing from the battle. Those killed were Jeremiah Peck from Hudson, Thomas Brightley of Blissfield and John Keegan and Homer Goodale, both of Deerfield (and both of whom survived for a few weeks after the battle before passing away). Coleman Dakin and Anson Farmer (from Palmyra) were captured by Rebel forces and later exchanged.

The wounded men included Patrick Keegan of Deerfield and Sylvester Smith of Morenci. Both men were officers of the regiment; Keegan served as first lieutenant, while Smith reached the rank of lieutenant colonel shortly before the battle. Keegan recovered from his wounds and would receive a promotion to the rank of captain for his actions in battle. Smith's wound, shot through the face, was more severe, and he returned to Michigan to work in the court-martial courts in Jackson.

GRANT MOVES SOUTH

With Confederate forces driven out of Tennessee, Union general U.S. Grant looked for a new target to take—one that would give the Union army control of the Mississippi River. Vicksburg, Mississippi, overlooked the Mississippi River, as the town is situated on a two-hundred-foot-tall bluff. Swamps and bayous to the north and south proved too much to march through. The only firm ground from which to approach the city was to the east, and Confederates constructed a maze of trenches, rifle pits and fortifications, making Vicksburg in 1863 the most heavily fortified city in the South. Two units with significant Lenawee ties—DeGolyer's Battery and Company B of the Forty-seventh Ohio—worked diligently with Grant's other assembled forces from February through July 1863 to win control of the strategic position.

After suffering through a wet winter and spring, the campaign began in earnest on April 29 with an attack near Grand Gulf, Mississippi. The distraction created by the ironclads on the river allowed Grant to move more than seventeen thousand men across the Mississippi from the west bank to the east bank. One of those units would be DeGolyer's Battery. At Bruinsburg, Mississippi, the battery crossed and marched toward Port Gibson. On the afternoon of May 1, the battery engaged the Rebel infantry and artillery. DeGolyer recalled, "I am proud to say that the Wolverines went in on their nerve, as they do anything else, and in a few minutes the rebels were driven from their position."[29]

Seeing the Rebels in retreat, DeGolyer's Battery and infantry supporting the artillery gave chase to the retreating forces. Shots rained down on enemy attempting to check Union advances, and soon the retreat became a rout. The battery lost only five men and six horses in the heavy fighting.

While DeGolyer's men and other Union forces marched along a route to place them in position to attack Vicksburg from the east, the men of the Forty-seventh Ohio worked at maintaining supplies for the Union forces. Company B of the Forty-seventh Ohio was made up of men from Lenawee County and, up to this point in the war, had not faced heavy conflict. Rather, they spent time guarding supply depots and fighting guerrilla forces.

To maintain supplies for the troops to the south of Vicksburg, Union naval forces "ran the gauntlet"—floating barges past the gun batteries defending the city. In April, two such missions were successful, but the naval forces did not want to attempt a third. The men of Company B of the Forty-seventh Ohio were happy to volunteer to try the mission.

On May 3, Captain William Ward and twelve other men from the Forty-seventh boarded the barges and the tow boat *George Sturgess* to attempt to float 400,000 rations to the troops below the city. The moonlight lit up the party as they floated down the Mississippi. When they reached the guns of Vicksburg, the bank lit up with cannon fire.

"Battery after battery opened on us as we came within range, until it seemed that the guns were being played upon like the keys of a piano, and to say that the rain of shot and shell was terrific but faintly describes the situation," wrote Captain William Ward after the action. The flotilla took on artillery and small arms fire for nearly forty-five minutes but had only one more small bend to navigate before reaching safety. Suddenly, a shell hit the boiler of the *George Sturgess*.[30]

The boiler exploded with a shower of burning coals, shards of metal and splinters of wood. Helpless to steer the barges, the men floated aimlessly. The

The grave site of Corporal Addison Hodges is located in the Ogden Cemetery. Hodges joined the Forty-seventh Ohio, Company B, and volunteered for the mission to run the batteries but, later that day, sold his spot to another man. When Captain Ward learned of this, both men joined the crew. Hodges would be awarded the Congressional Medal of Honor for the risky mission. *Courtesy of Kara Lennard.*

barges ignited, and the volunteers from the Forty-seventh Ohio dove into the water for safety. Four were able to escape, while the remainder were fished out of the water by Confederate forces and became prisoners of war.

Grant would not be deterred, even after losing the rations for the attackers marching to reach the east side of Vicksburg. On May 12, the Seventeenth Army Corps (of which DeGolyer's Battery was a member) came into contact with a large Confederate force. Hearing the sounds of action, DeGolyer and his men made haste toward the sound of the fight. The battery found the enemy in force along the steep banks of Fourteen Mile Creek. A force of Confederate infantry made a flanking attack during a lull in the fighting that took the Union forces by surprise. DeGolyer's Battery fought a savage fight to maintain control of its guns as enemy forces nearly overwhelmed it.

Private Orrin R. Smith, from Medina, sustained injuries to his head and chest when a solid-shot cannonball passed within a few inches of him. The concussion from the shell caused long-term injuries, and on January 25, 1864, he would receive a medical discharge.

On May 16, Grant learned that Confederate troops had consolidated in an attempt to defeat his army. The massed Rebel troops set up a defensive line around the homestead of Sidney S. Champion. Again, Samuel DeGolyer and his troops performed admirably during the fight and chased after the fleeing Rebels. The *Cincinnati Commercial* newspaper reported, "Captain DeGolyer is spoken of in the highest terms by his superior officers."[31]

General U.S. Grant attempted to take Vicksburg by force on May 19. That morning, DeGolyer's men fired on the entrenchments for four hours before Sherman's Corps, including the Forty-seventh Ohio, stormed the works. Within minutes, the Yankees came retreating back across the field after suffering heavy casualties.

Three days later, Grant tried again to take Vicksburg by force. Members of the Forty-seventh Ohio joined in what became known at the "forlorn hope" attack. A select group of men volunteered to run before the assaulting force with ladders and planks to form a bridge over the ditches guarding the fortresses of Vicksburg. The men of the party knew certain death awaited them, as they were ripe targets for Rebel sharpshooters. The attack failed, as the ladders and planks were not long enough to bridge the fortifications. Federal forces, including the Forty-seventh Ohio, pushed forward as far as they could and waited for darkness to retreat across the open field.

May 24 saw members of DeGolyer's Battery moving the battery guns closer to Rebel lines. The lead guns were within a few yards of the fortifications protecting Vicksburg. Rebel sharpshooters began firing on the exposed battery, and in the process Corporal John S. Richmond of Hudson was hit. The barrel maker was hit in his right thigh, and the bullet exited just above his knee. Richmond survived and would be discharged at the end of his term of enlistment. The guns were pulled back soon after.

The opposing force from DeGolyer's Battery was the Third Louisiana Infantry. Its men were issued new Enfield rifles on May 28. The regiment tested the accuracy of its new weapons with great zeal—and the men of the battery took notice, scrambling from around the guns to the rifle pits for shelter. Just behind the front line, Samuel DeGolyer was under a tent fly resting, taking shelter from the midday sun. Without warning, DeGolyer was hit in the thigh by a rifle shot. The musket ball entered the upper third of his thigh near the groin. Field surgeons knew the severity of the wound and shipped DeGolyer to the new hospital boat, the USS *Red Rover*. Under constant care, DeGolyer appeared to recover.

Kate DeGolyer joined her husband in early June. Mrs. DeGolyer made plans in mid-July to bring her husband home to Hudson. On July 30, the DeGolyers did just that. The August 1 edition of the *Hudson Gazette* wrote, "We are pleased to learn that he is quite comfortable at the present writing, but he needs rest and ought not to be disturbed by visitors." His condition began to deteriorate on August 4, and in the evening on August 7, DeGolyer passed away.

The siege at Vicksburg continued. The Federals waited out in the southern heat, boredom broken only by two-hour barrages on the town or the occasional *pop, pop, pop* from sharpshooters. On June 1, James Webster from Rollin Township, serving in DeGolyer's Battery, received a gunshot wound to the mouth from a sharpshooter but would survive and serve until the end of the war. Isaac Crawford, of the same unit and from Addison, became ill as disease set in around the camps. Crawford would die on August 24.

On July 4, Vicksburg surrendered. The men of the Eighth Michigan Battery and the Forty-seventh Ohio, Company B, entered the town and toured the ruined city. The men were weary from forty-seven days of marching, fighting and siege work. Now they were on orders to guard the city and prisoners.

Following the fall of Vicksburg, Grant was free to deal with a growing Rebel threat in his rear, near Jackson, Mississippi. The Second Michigan (as well as the Seventeenth Michigan) had been transferred to the western theater to bolster the manpower of Grant's forces. William Humphrey had been promoted to colonel of the Second Michigan. Both regiments were part of the Ninth Army Corps that battled for control of the city. Facing superior forces, the Rebels abandoned the town in the middle of the night.

WAR IN THE EAST

The Fourth Michigan, after participating in Fredericksburg in December 1862, did little heavy fighting. At Chancellorsville in May 1863, the Fourth skirmished with Confederates but did not see the heavy action other Federal units did. On May 25 and 26, Michigan governor Austin Blair visited the camps of Michigan regiments, including the Fourth. A few days later, the men of the Fourth, along with the rest of the Army of the Potomac, began to move north toward Maryland.

Right: Dr. Luther French of Hudson entered into service in the Fourth Michigan Infantry in August 1862. In May 1863, Dr. French replaced Dr. David Chamberlain as the regimental surgeon. Dr. French left the unit in late May 1863 due to his declining health. *Courtesy of Hudson Museum.*

Below: A drawing of the Fourth Michigan engaged with the enemy in the woods near the "Wheatfield" at Gettysburg, by Lieutenant Charles Gruner. *Courtesy of Hudson Museum.*

The Federal troops shadowed the northern movement of Lee's Confederate army. Late in June, the two armies maneuvered around each other in the hills of Maryland and Pennsylvania, with the Federal army trying to maintain position between Lee and Washington, D.C. The two forces converged at the small town of Gettysburg on July 1, 1863.

The Fourth Michigan arrived on the field of battle on July 2, 1863. At three o'clock in the afternoon, the soldiers found themselves in an area of high ground they called Powers Hill on the left of the Union line. Across from them, Confederate forces began to mass for attack. Major General Winfield Hancock called for reinforcements on the Union left flank. The men of the Fourth marched toward Trostle's Woods and a small wheat field.

Colonel Sweitzer (commander of the brigade to which the Fourth Michigan belonged) maneuvered the troops toward the woods where he thought they would link up with Union troops. As the men of the Fourth marched through the "Wheatfield," stray shots began to hit the regiment, informing the men there were no friendly forces in the woods. Within an instant, Rebel troops appeared on the right of the Fourth. With the attention of the regiment focused on the threat in the front, the Rebel attack on the right smashed into the exposed flank.

Volleys from the enemy poured into the front, right and rear of the Fourth Michigan. Confederate forces then rushed the staggered men. William Tolford of Hudson wrote of the "severe cross fire" the men were exposed to. As the Fourth withdrew from the field toward the safety of Union reserves, the scene was horrifying.[32]

Lieutenant Orvey Barrett from Adrian received a severe wound to the leg, and he fell to the ground. The battle swirled around him, and a Rebel soldier approached to bayonet him. Fortunately, a Confederate officer stopped the soldier from performing the act, saving Barrett's life. As the Union and Confederate lines surged back and forth, Barrett recalled, "They had no time to scoop any of the wounded as they had all they could attend to in getting out themselves."[33]

As night fell, the fighting ended, and the men of the Fourth Michigan regrouped. The regiment had gone into action with 342 men, and only 139 remained. Albert Boies from Hudson was one of the wounded men—missing two fingers on the right hand—and evaded Confederate capture, sneaking away from his Rebel captors after dark. Frank Clark of Morenci suffered a shattered leg. The most memorable loss was that of their colonel, Harrison Jeffords. Newspapers across southeastern Lower Michigan reported:

Martin Pennock of Tecumseh has an unusual grave: "victim of rebel cruelty." Many of the men from the Fourth who were captured at Gettysburg would be held at Libby Prison. They were deprived of their shoes, coats and other articles of clothing, leaving the men with only a shirt, pants and socks. *Courtesy of Kara Lennard.*

> *It was from a bayonet thrust that Col Jefferds* [sic] *fell. It was in the thickest of the fight. A rebel officer had seized the regimental colors. Col Jefferds shot the rebel dead. . . . A rebel bayonet pierced his vitals, and he fell dead, his hand still clutching the flagstaff.*[34]

The Fourth Michigan was not the only unit with Lenawee County connections to suffer on the afternoon of July 2. Company C of the First United States Sharpshooters boasted mainly men from Michigan, including

A boulder marking the grave site of General George A. Custer's horse, Don Juan. The Confederate Thoroughbred horse, which bolted past the presidential review stand in 1865, was sent to Lieutenant Elliott Gray's horse farm in Tecumseh. When the horse died in 1866, Gray buried the steed near the entrance of his farm on Russel Road. The boulder marker was placed on the site by the current landowner, Brady Sand and Gravel. *Courtesy of Kara Lennard.*

several from the Hudson area. Stationed in the area of Little Round Top, the unit assisted in fending off repeated Confederate attacks throughout the late afternoon and evening. Seven members of the company were killed in the fight, including Harrison Higby and George Sheldon of Hudson, as well as Simon Roosa from Medina.

On July 3, Confederate forces renewed the attack with a grand charge in an attempt to break the center of the Union lines. Known in history as Pickett's Charge (named for Confederate general George Pickett), it would fail, with Union forces repulsing the attack. A lesser-known action took place at the same time; had Federal cavalry forces not succeeded in checking an attack by Rebel cavalry aimed at the rear of the Union lines, July 3 would have ended very differently.

The Seventh Michigan Volunteer Cavalry played a role in this defense. The unit organized in late 1862 from volunteers across the state of Michigan. Several men from Lenawee County joined the unit, including Elliott Gray from Tecumseh. In the spring of 1863, the unit moved to Washington, D.C.

In late June, the Seventh Michigan joined what would become known as the Michigan Cavalry Brigade under the command of General George Armstrong Custer. On July 3, Custer recalled the actions of the unit:

> *At once I ordered the Seventh Michigan Cavalry to charge the advancing column of the enemy. The ground was very unfavorable for the maneuvering of cavalry, but, despite all obstacles, the regiment boldly advanced to the assault, which was executed in splendid style, the enemy being driven from field to field, until our advance reached a high and unbroken fence, behind which the enemy was strongly posted. Nothing daunted, Colonel Mann, followed by the main body of his regiment, bravely rode up to the fence, discharging revolvers in the very face of the foe.*[35]

The Confederate attempt to turn the Union lines and attack the rear had failed, mainly through the work of the Michigan Cavalry Brigade and the Seventh Michigan. The unit spent the days after the battle chasing Lee's retreating forces back across the Potomac River and into Northern Virginia. At Falling Waters, Maryland, on July 14, the Seventh Cavalry engaged the Fifty-fifth Virginia, capturing four hundred prisoners and the battle flag of the unit. During the action, Harlan B. Cochran of Palmyra was killed.

RELIEF WORK

Laura Haviland continued to run the Raisin Institute until 1863. In the late spring, Haviland offered her services as a nurse to the government to aid the sick and wounded Union soldiers. Her services were accepted by Michigan governor Austin Blair, and Fernando Beaman aided Haviland in weeding through Federal government paperwork and wartime transportation issues. Haviland arrived near Island Number 10 and began working with the Freedmen's Bureau to care for ex-slaves now trying to figure out how to survive in the new South. One of the primary concerns was clothing. Haviland left Lenawee County with large trunks of donated supplies for the needs of soldiers and others in the South. She reported on her works near Island Number 10:

> *Soon we were beside the boxes in our commissary tent measuring, fitting, and handing out, when up stepped the little fellow of eight summers with the tall man's pants, rolled over and over at the bottom, with one suspender tied around him, the other placed over his shoulder to hold them on. His eyes sparkled as a new suit was thrown over his arm; calling out, "See here, Johnnie, what I got!" "Yes, look at mine!" was the quick reply, while on the other side stood a little girl who exclaimed, in surprise, "Oh, Milla, my dress has a pocket, and see what I found," as she drew out a rag doll two inches long. Then a dozen other little girls instituted a search and found similar treasures, which I recognized as coming from certain little girls in Hudson, Michigan.*[36]

Haviland had returned to Michigan by June 1. She went to work organizing a Freedmen's Bureau to collect supplies for a fall trip to the South. By mid-September, Haviland again found herself in the South, near Vicksburg, Mississippi. Her time here was spent assisting the Federal army hospitals, distributing clothing to freed slaves and performing mission work, including distribution of Bibles.

Haviland was not the only woman from Lenawee County to serve the war effort as a nurse in the theaters of war. Marion Bannister from Tecumseh served as one, as well, and is only one of two women in the state who received a pension for her service after the war.

In Hudson, Mrs. Sarah Evens traveled to Washington to nurse her husband, George, back to health after he was wounded at the first Battle of Bull Run. On April 16, 1862, Evens gathered other friends in Washington to decorate the graves of Michigan soldiers in the local cemeteries. The next year, on the same date, they repeated the act at Fredericksburg. Mrs. Evens may have contributed to the idea of Decoration Day, now known as Memorial Day, from her act of honoring Michigan's dead.

Back in Lenawee County, residents supported the war effort through the collection of home goods for shipment to the Sanitary Commission offices

The grave site of Marion Bannister, located in Brookside Cemetery in Tecumseh. Bannister was one of a handful of women from Lenawee County who served as nurses in field hospitals during the Civil War. *Courtesy of Kara Lennard.*

in Chicago, Illinois, for distribution in the theaters of war. Goods like jams, jellies, pickles, dried apples, socks and other articles of clothing were vital to the group's efforts. Besides the material goods, the Sanitary Commission needed cash donations to ensure the products were able to be shipped. Local groups of women worked in hosting entertainment, church fairs or other events that collected funds and goods.

By October 1863, participation in the Sanitary Commission efforts in Lenawee had lagged in Tecumseh. A late fall concert raised only a little over seven dollars for the purchase of fabric for clothing for needy soldiers. Donations of foodstuffs were lower than they had been in other months as well. In a terse letter to the editor of the *Tecumseh Herald* published on October 15, Mrs. C.M. Bissell wrote:

> *I hope those who are staying here and enjoying the comforts, yea luxuries of home and the society of their families will think of the brave men who have left the dear ones and gone forth, many of them never to return again; those that have gone will endure many hardships and greater privations than*

any of you who stay at home can ever know. Give of your substance more liberally than you have yet done and I can assure you that it will not go into the bank and be kept from the neey [sic] *soldier for six months, but used judiciously and a report made out accordingly.*

AFRICAN AMERICAN TROOPS JOIN THE FIGHT

President Abraham Lincoln announced his intention to issue the Emancipation Proclamation on September 22, 1862. The proclamation went into effect in all Confederate-controlled areas on January 1, 1863. Massachusetts governor John Andrew saw this as an opportunity to enlist a regiment of African American troops for the war effort. Andrew began petitioning the War Department in April 1862 to authorize black troops to fight in the war. In March 1863, Andrew selected Robert Gould Shaw to serve as commander of the Fifty-fourth Massachusetts.

The grave site of Benjamin Ross, a member of the Fifty-fourth Massachusetts. Benjamin enlisted in the unit in early 1863. The famous regiment is portrayed in the Hollywood movie *Glory*. *Courtesy of Kara Lennard.*

Enlistments for the regiment came from all over the Union. The idea of enlisting a regiment of African American troops appealed to antislavery advocates across the country. Leaders in free black communities petitioned Massachusetts to allow their men to enlist. Lenawee County was no different.

In early April 1863, a recruiting officer came to Adrian seeking volunteers for the Fifty-fourth Massachusetts. Nine African Americans enlisted. The men included James Coleman, John Coleman, George W. Dorsey, James Jackson, Birney Johnson, Benjamin Ross (from Tecumseh), Daniel Ross, Nelson Payne and Henry Steward. Recruitment for the regiment was so strong that Massachusetts added another regiment of all African American soldiers: the Fifty-fifth Massachusetts. John Jackson of Adrian enlisted in this regiment and served as a first sergeant.

The Fifty-fourth Massachusetts gained notoriety for the assault on the Confederate position known as Fort Wagner outside Charleston, South Carolina. The attack on the heavily fortified position caused the regiment to lose 272 men killed, wounded or captured, including Colonel Shaw. James and John Coleman were 2 of those wounded in the battle. James Coleman would be discharged on May 13, 1864, for his wounds. John Coleman returned to the Fifty-fourth and served out the war.

Top: The grave site of James Colemen, also a member of the Fifty-fourth Massachusetts, who enlisted in early 1863. *Courtesy of Kara Lennard.*

Right: Henry F. Steward was one of the local African Americans to enlist in the Civil War. He fought for the Union and to end slavery. *Courtesy of Massachusetts State Historical Society.*

The regiment also lost men to disease. George W. Dorsey died while in the hospital on Morris Island in South Carolina. The most notable Lenawee soldier in the Fifty-fourth was Sergeant Henry Steward of Company E. He rose to the rank of sergeant and died of disease on September 27, 1863, while the unit stayed on Morris Island.

Massachusetts's success in raising an African American regiment led to both the Federal government and Northern states raising regiments. In Michigan, recruitment began for the 1st Michigan Colored Infantry in July. The regiment would be turned over to the Federal government and became known as the 102nd United States Colored Troops (USCT).

The nearly 900-man regiment left the state in March 1864 and eventually ended up in South Carolina. The unit would see action in both South Carolina and Florida in battles and skirmishes. Over 1,400 men would serve in the regiment, with 23 Lenawee residents, including Benjamin James from Seneca, Robert Flynn of Tecumseh and John B. Brown of Hudson (who obtained the rank of corporal).

Several soldiers from around Lenawee offered to command the African American troops. The men had to pass a rigorous examination to become officers. Daniel A. Bennett of Morenci was one such man who passed the tests, transferring from the Eleventh Michigan in January 1864 to become a second lieutenant in the Fifteenth USCT.

CHATTANOOGA AND THE WAR IN TENNESSEE

After Vicksburg, the western theater of war was quiet while Union forces reorganized and sought out new military targets. The Eleventh Michigan had not participated in many actions after the battle at Stones River and spent most of 1863 on provost duty in Tennessee. In the late summer, a new target had been acquired—a Confederate force under the command of Braxton Bragg near Chattanooga—and the Eleventh Michigan was one of the units selected to destroy that army.

In September, members of the Eleventh Michigan found themselves in the lead of the Union forces creeping to Chattanooga. At a place known as Davis Cross Roads, the Eleventh engaged elements of Bragg's army in Dade County, Georgia. While the maneuvers were merely the two sides probing each other's strengths, it was still dangerous work for the men. David Edwards of Medina would be killed when shot through the cheek and neck.

Oliver W. Brockway of Morenci would end up captured by the Rebels. He would be sent to Andersonville Prison, where he would die.

The deadly tango of the two armies continued for the next week. On September 19, the two armies engaged in a full-scale battle that would become known as Chickamauga. The Eleventh Michigan participated as a veteran unit in some of the tightest portions of the battle. The regiment was acknowledged by General Rosencrans when it was called on to check a Confederate advance. "Make it warm for them, Michigan boys. . . . I know you will."[37]

The next day (September 20), the men of the Eleventh Michigan were placed on top of Snodgrass Hill, a key position for the Union forces that hoped to hold off the Confederate attack. The heavy fighting that the men of the regiment had done over the last thirty-six hours was beginning to take a toll. The rifles of the men were fouled, making it difficult to load the weapons. Furthermore, the men of the Eleventh were running dangerously low on ammunition, causing them to scour the bodies of fallen men for more munitions.

Over the course of the afternoon, the fighting became savage. Hand-to-hand combat broke out as the two lines came into contact with each other. The veteran men of both sides commented that they had never seen anything like it. "A contest ensued, which in its fierceness and duration has few parallels," reported General Joseph B. Kernshaw after the battle. It was a testament to the ferocity of the fight, as two months' prior, Kernshaw had fought in the peach orchard at Gettysburg with his command suffering 50 percent casualties.[38]

The Eleventh Michigan was outnumbered but would not be outfought. At one point, the regiment was fighting three Confederate troops for every one Michigander. In the end, it would prevail and hold the position, allowing the Federal army to slip back to the safety of Chattanooga.

While events transpired in Chattanooga, Knoxville became a focus for the Confederates. The area was not only a key rail hub linking the western theater of war to the eastern theater, but it also held strong Union supporters and rich natural resources. The Union high command sent General Ambrose Burnside's Ninth Corps to hold this vital area.

The Ninth Corps included the Second Michigan, Seventeenth Michigan and Twentieth Michigan; all three units were in the same brigade and were under the command of William Humphries. Humphries would work well with the commanders of the Seventeenth and Twentieth Michigan, as Loren Comstock led the Seventeenth and William Huntington Smith (of Adrian) was a colonel of the Twentieth.

Humphries's outfit served as the rear guard of Burnside's corps. Longstreet planned to travel to Sweetwater, Tennessee, where he would take on supplies for the campaign and hopefully out race Union forces to Knoxville. From November 12 to 15, the men from Michigan, under command of Humphries, skirmished with the Rebels in an attempt to slow their advance while Burnside readied Knoxville.

November 16 found the two armies contesting the small crossroads of Campbell's Station. The road to Knoxville met the road from Chattanooga here, and Union forces held the ground. Longstreet ordered attacks on both Union flanks, hoping to overwhelm the troops. The Federal troops held steady, buying time for an organized withdrawal back to the forts of Knoxville. In the action, William Huntington Smith would be shot through the head and killed.[39]

The Confederate failure at Campbell's Station left General Longstreet with the only option of laying siege to Knoxville. Without siege guns, running low on supplies and not having the manpower to effectively encircle the area, Longstreet's plan was on shaky ground. Snipers from both sides traded fire. The Seventeenth Michigan fought with the deadly marksmen on a regular basis. On November 20, the men of the Seventeenth charged an abandoned house used by the Confederate marksmen and burned it—a feat that won the Medal of Honor for three men of the regiment. But the snipers continued. On November 25, Loren Comstock would be hit in the chest by a sniper's bullet.

Comstock would be buried in Knoxville but not left there. Charles D. Todd of Adrian, a first lieutenant in Company D, was charged with locating the burial site of Comstock and other members of the Seventeenth killed in Knoxville. Todd detailed a party to locate and dig up their comrades for transport back to Michigan. He wrote in his diary that they were able only to remove Comstock's remains and stayed on guard with the body for forty-eight hours before the casket was shipped back to Mrs. Comstock.[40]

5

1864: The War Drags On

For two and a half years, news of the war greeted residents of Lenawee County. The biggest story of January 1864 was the massive winter storm that overtook the area on New Year's Eve and Day. Franklin Dewey of Cambridge Township recalled the nasty storm nearly seventy years after the day:

> *The evening* [New Year's Eve] *was warm and foggy. . . . My father had a thermometer on the porch. The mercury stood at seventy. . . . About two in the morning we were awakened by the whistling and the wild howling of the winds, the frightful roaring of the tempest. At sixty or seventy miles an hour, and if possible, much more, it was streaking across the country; the air full, not of snow, but of sharp, keen, cutting ice that struck the face like fine shot fired from a gun.*[41]

Dewey reported that the temperature plummeted nearly ninety degrees in a matter of six hours, finally settling at around twenty degrees below zero. A large gathering of partygoers at the brick tavern at Cambridge Junction (near Walker Tavern) found themselves in a bad position. The rooms were booked full at the tavern, and as the evening drew on, many attempted to drive home, only to be frostbitten. Dewey recalled a brother and sister who attempted to rush home down the Monroe Pike (modern-day M-50). The sister perished from the cold while her brother suffered extreme frostbite.

The weather was equally poor for Lenawee troops in the field. The James River at Richmond, Virginia, froze over solid. Union prisoners incarcerated at Belle Isle froze to death. In Arkansas, a Federal force—men, horses and artillery—crossed the White River by walking over the frozen waterway. Members of the Forty-seventh Ohio at Chattanooga recalled that at noon, ink taken from the bottle by the nib would freeze before being used on paper.[42]

RECRUITING AND DRAFTING

The Congress of the United States authorized military drafts starting in March 1863. Lenawee County would be spared the randomness of drafts throughout the majority of the year. Signs of resistance to the war could be identified in the closing months of 1863. In the Fourth Michigan, the question of reenlistment came up when Major Jarius Hall of Adrian read an offer to the men whose three-year enlistment would be up in June. If they reenlisted for three more years, they would be designated "Veteran Volunteers," be able to collect a $300 bounty and go home on furlough for thirty days.

It was a hard sell. Many of the men had had enough of fighting; the long, cold nights lying on the ground; and the physical toll of being a soldier. Henry Seage of Hudson was one of the twenty men who jumped at the offer. After a few days, he recanted his enlistment. Seage recalled, "Major and Colonel distributed whiskey among the vets and an awful drunk ensued. A fine way to get men to enlist." Some men did refuse to serve any longer than the three-year initial term, including Silas Sadler of Company G, who wished to return home to his parents and Tecumseh.[43]

The inability to get reenlistments meant that the men back at home needed to volunteer to fill the quotas for the towns, villages and townships. The first draft for Lenawee County would occur on November 2, 1863, for the quota of troops to be filled by January 1864. L.G. Berry and H. Underwood of Adrian both served as the officials for the draft.

The first draft drew 172 names for service. The only areas that met the quota were Tecumseh and Hudson. One member of the crowd, when his neighbor was drawn from the hopper, shouted, "Give it another turn old man—I don't want to go!"[44]

Local towns and villages spent the next few months gathering recruits and soliciting funds to pay out bounties that would ensure the draft would not have to occur again. For example, Tecumseh worked in the first part of 1864 to raise $7,500 to procure volunteers and pay bounties.

Grant Comes East

In early March, the Army of the Potomac came under control of General Ulysses Grant. Organizing the army, as well as dealing with the weather, delayed any offensive movement in Virginia until the first of May. The army moved toward Richmond, and by May 4 the men of the Second, Fourth and Seventeenth Michigan found themselves near Chancellorsville in an area known as the Wilderness.

On May 5, Union and Confederate forces met in battle along the Orange Turnpike near the Wilderness Tavern. In the afternoon, the men of the Fourth Michigan entered the fray in a piece of open land known as Saunders Field. A sharp fight ensued, and the Fourth Michigan and elements of the Fifth Corps would be beaten back with heavy losses, including William Tolford of Hudson, who was killed in action, and Colonel Lumbard, whose wound would prove to be fatal (the third colonel of the regiment killed in action). The remainder of the Battle of the Wilderness for the Fourth Regiment was spent behind breastworks in relatively quiet sectors of the field.

LeRoy Mead enlisted in the Fourth Michigan Infantry, Company G, as a corporal when the war commenced. By May 1864, Mead served as second lieutenant in charge of Company K. Mead was wounded at the Wilderness and left the service at the end of his three-year enlistment. *Courtesy of Bentley Historical Library.*

On May 8, Grant maneuvered his army south

William Humphrey, a member of the Second Michigan Infantry, rose from the rank of captain to brevet brigadier general (for bravery in action at Spotsylvania). When he returned to Adrian, Humphrey worked as an editor, auditor general and warden. *Courtesy of the U.S. Army War College Library.*

to engage Lee, whose army dug in near Spotsylvania Court House. The Fourth Michigan participated in skirmishes for the next five days and lost 10 killed and nearly 30 wounded in the action. The regiment now numbered around 159 men, down from the nearly 1,030 who had left Adrian in 1861.

The Second and Seventeenth Michigan entered the fight on May 12. Grant sought an opportunity to draw Lee out from his entrenchments and fight in the open. His plan was to have the men of the Ninth Corps attack. Colonel William Humphrey (from Adrian) commanded the First Brigade of the Third Division, the unit of which the Second Michigan was a part. As the Union attack was organized to be launched, Confederate troops surged forward in an attack. Union forces switched from offense to defense. Humphrey wrote that nearly every man in the unit was killed or wounded, but the men of the Second Michigan had checked the advance.

Farther along the Federal lines, the Seventeenth Michigan would bear the brunt of a Confederate division's attack. The colonel of the Seventeenth learned of the attack when a private shouted that the Confederates were approaching. An incoming shell killed the private and hurled him into the colonel, who fell facedown as the Rebels poured into the area. In the mêlée, the majority of the Seventeenth Michigan managed to avoid capture. One man who was not so lucky was William R. McMire of Adrian. He was captured and sent to Andersonville Prison, where he died of disease on October 27.

On May 23, the Fourth Michigan engaged the enemy at the North Anna River and was driven back to hastily prepared entrenchments. The next day,

Grant maneuvered forces to renew the attack. He selected General Burnside to lead the attack, and in turn, Burnside selected the Seventeenth Michigan (along with the Twenty-second Massachusetts) to lead the assault. Federal artillery opened to provide cover to get the men across Ox Ford. Just as the men of the Seventeenth prepared to rush the Confederate entrenchment, the plan of attack changed. A soldier from the First Michigan Sharpshooters wrote, "Thank God General Burnside countermanded the order."[45]

The Second Michigan followed the actions of Grant as the Army of the Potomac moved south and fought Lee. Along the way, the Second gained new troops to replace those who had been killed or whose terms of service were coming to an end. One such recruit was Faron Anderson from Tecumseh.

Anderson had tried to join the military several times; however, his father had prevented him from doing so. Finally, in March, his father relented, and Faron enlisted in Company B of the Second Michigan for three years. Within weeks, Anderson wrote home, stating:

> *Do not enlist if you know when you are well off it is a hard life at best for that last long march that we made some of the men layed down and died you ought to have seen us that day that we rested we were all dust and my feet were all blistered.*[46]

On June 2, members of the Fourth Michigan engaged the Rebels near Cold Harbor. It was familiar ground for the men near Mechanicsville, and they remembered the terrible toll the fighting had taken just two years earlier. The next day, the Fourth moved out in a skirmish line to engage Confederate forces while Grant focused his attacks on the south end of the Rebel entrenchments. Rebel artillery raked the Federal line and made the position uncomfortable for the men.

After the Union army's failure at Cold Harbor, Grant marched on Petersburg in an attempt to get around Lee and Richmond. Confederate forces arrived just in time to prevent the fall of the city and raced to set up stronger defensive lines. For the men of the Fourth, they waited for their enlistments to end.

On June 18, just two days before the end of many of the men's enlistments, Grant ordered a general assault of the Confederate lines. Colonel Jacob Sweitzer, the brigade commander, promised the Fourth that he would call on them only if the need was urgent. Harrison Daniels (of Tecumseh) recalled that Sweitzer "wanted to know if the enemy pushed him if we would stand by him. . . . We all said 'Yes!'"[47]

Throughout the day of the eighteenth, the men of the Fourth Regiment listened to the din of the battle and watched the wounded stream back to the rear. At around 6:00 p.m., the dreaded order came for the men to march to the battlefront. The Fourth came onto line near dusk to relieve another regiment and extend the breastworks. Working quietly through the night, the men waited for morning.

At 10:00 a.m. on June 19, the Fourth Michigan was relieved by a regiment, and many of the men would be headed home in just a few short hours. But first, the men needed to escape the Confederate sharpshooters and make it to the safety of the Union rear. Daniels recalled, "We were under fire all the way down the hill, the dirt flew about my feet."[48] Two men would be hit from the fire; William Palmer of Ridgeway was killed (Palmer was one of the few men who had reenlisted for another term of service).

On June 20, the Fourth Michigan departed for Detroit. Over 150 men boarded the mail steamer at City Point, Virginia, bound for home. It took the men five days to reach Detroit. When they arrived, there were no citizens to greet them. The barracks that were to house the men of the unit were deemed unfit for habitation, so the men slept on the sidewalks, causing residents of the neighborhood to draw their curtains. Moses Luce, a Hillsdale College student who would win a Medal of Honor for his actions in the Battle at Spotsylvania, quipped, "The soldier now was nobody and I was already a vagrant."[49]

On June 30, the men were formally mustered out of service. The ladies of Adrian, who three years earlier had presented a flag to the Fourth, requested that the veterans come and celebrate the Fourth of July with them. Nearly 120 men of the old Fourth gathered in Adrian to return the tattered flag of the regiment to the ladies of Adrian. Dr. John Watts, who had served as the assistant surgeon, gave the ladies and those gathered thanks on behalf of the men of the regiment.

For the nearly 170 members of the Fourth Michigan whose terms of enlistment were not expired, the war dragged on. Without many officers and no surgeon or quartermaster, the unit was dissolved and joined the First Michigan Regiment.

REORGANIZED FOURTH MICHIGAN

In the late summer and early fall, recruiters worked to fill a regiment of troops to serve the war effort. Word soon came that the new regiment would be known as the reorganized Fourth and that it was to gather on the grounds of Adrian College for training. The news sent Adrian into a flurry of activity. Charles Cleveland, who had supplied food for the original regiment, won the contract to feed the new regiment.

By October, nearly 750 men were training in Adrian. The town welcomed them as it had welcomed the original Fourth. Sunday was a lively day at camp as visitors watched the men work at the art of war. On October 22, the men of the Reorganized Fourth broke camp and headed south for Nashville, Tennessee. The new regiment would serve in Alabama and Texas throughout the remainder of the war.

Sherman Attacks in the West

For the men of the Eleventh Michigan, Fifteenth Michigan, Eighteenth Michigan and DeGolyer's Battery, the spring of 1864 brought little in the way of action. For the most part, men of western theater units spent time performing guard duty, brushing up on drill, refitting equipment and probing areas for "bushwhackers" (irregular Confederate soldiers). With General Grant moving to the eastern theater, General William Tecumseh Sherman took over operations in the western theater. By May, Sherman had initiated his plan with Atlanta, Georgia, as the target.

For troops like DeGolyer's Battery, stationed near Vicksburg, Mississippi, this meant marching to northern Georgia to get in position. Slowly, Sherman's force grew. The two armies engaged in skirmishes and probes as Sherman pressed toward Atlanta.

One man from Hudson, Lindley R. Harkness, partook in a risky operation during the early phase of the Atlanta campaign. Commissary Sergeant Harkness of the Eleventh Michigan was detailed to act as a scout behind Confederate lines. Dressed as a civilian, he was to gather information about the strength and movements of the Rebel forces. Thankfully, he safely completed the mission without incident, for if he were caught, he would have been executed.

The month of June was wet, forcing the Union attackers to wait for better weather. In places along the front lines, the enemy could be seen barely one hundred yards away. The Eleventh Michigan spent weeks on the front line as skirmishers battling Confederates. The spirit of the men was never higher, as they knew it was only a matter of time before the Rebel city would fall.

Wesley Marlatt of Dover Township joined the Eighteenth Michigan Infantry. Marlatt died of disease in Nashville on December 2, 1864. *Courtesy of Lenawee County Historical Museum.*

An order came on July 4 for the Eleventh Michigan to engage the enemy in a distraction to allow its fellow units to attempt a flanking maneuver. The Eleventh managed to drive the Confederates from their entrenchments at a cost. In the fight, the Eleventh's colonel would be wounded. Overall command of the regiment fell to Captain Patrick Keegan of Deerfield.

On July 22, Confederate general John Bell Hood saw an opportunity to smash a portion of Sherman's troops. For DeGolyer's Battery, this meant a hard-pressed fight. As the Confederates attacked in a wave, the battery was forced to fight in a retreating manner. One of the officers of the battery recalled the men's fighting spirit:

> *It was just the place to form a line of battle. Some general officer may have given an order to stop there. My own belief always has been that the boys did it of their own accord. They had been in so many fights that they did not need a general to tell them where and when to stop running and begin shooting.*[50]

It was at this juncture that Private Nathaniel Woodfield from Tecumseh suffered a wound to his side. Woodfield was riding one of the battery horses when his foot caught on a sapling, throwing him forward onto the pommel. This caused a rupture near his ribs.

The ground was a good spot for a defensive fight. Fire from the cannon checked Confederate infantry and silenced opposing artillery. Moving to the aid of the battery was the Fifteenth Michigan Infantry. The men from the Fifteenth hit the remaining Rebel attackers and sent them reeling. In the process of the counterattack, the Fifteenth captured a stand of Rebel colors and took a few prisoners. In this position, two more Confederate attacks were fended off.

The Forty-seventh Ohio, Company B, fought savagely on July 22 as well. Charged with other units from the Fifteenth Corps to aid in retaking the lost Union lines, the Forty-seventh Ohio charged headlong into the fray. It would be a costly attack for the men from Lenawee. Joseph Sudburogh, Charles Derby and George Rider were all killed in action. Henry Nash, who risked his life at Vicksburg by floating down the river batteries, was one of four members of Company B captured by Rebel forces.

In early August, Sherman moved to cut off the rail line that supplied the Confederate defenders in Atlanta. The Eleventh Michigan moved to the extreme right of the Federal lines and into camp at Utoy Creek. On August 7, the men looked across an open field toward the dual lines of Rebel entrenchments and waited.

The order to attack came at 1:00 p.m. The Eleventh Michigan learned that the plan of attack positioned them to the right of the attacking force. This would expose the men to fire in both the front and the right during the nearly quarter mile of open ground they would need to cross.

The men of the Eleventh balked at the assignment. Their terms of enlistment would be up in just a few days, and they saw the attack on the strong position as useless. When the other regiments sprang out of the entrenchments toward the enemy, the Eleventh stood fast.

The grave site of Corporal Henry Nash in the Palmyra Village Cemetery. Nash won the Medal of Honor for his actions at Vicksburg, awarded to him in 1909. *Courtesy of Kara Lennard.*

Lieutenant Colonel Henry Mudge stood atop the trench and shamed the men forward with a short speech that ended with: "Let not a man shirk from duty!"[51]

Nearly all the men poured out of the trench and stormed across the field. A few remained behind, including the acting colonel, Patrick Keegan. Those who made the charge scampered up the hill and entered the Rebel position. Hundreds of Confederates were overrun and forced to retreat.

The Eleventh regrouped and looked toward the reserve line of Confederates, 150 yards away. A face-off occurred with the Federal troops not willing to go any farther and the Rebels refusing to budge. The Eleventh held this position for a few days before being relieved and sent to Chattanooga to be discharged.

Sherman slowly began to encircle Atlanta and laid siege to the city. DeGolyer's Battery would move positions a few times but focused on throwing shot and shell into the city. The men of the battery estimated that they fired nearly five thousand shells at the Rebel defenses.

After the fall of Atlanta, DeGolyer's Battery was nearly used up. The unit had been issued new guns after Vicksburg but was still using the same caissons and wagons it had been issued in 1862. For that reason, Sherman ordered the unit to relocate to Nashville rather than participate in the "March to the Sea." The men served out the remainder of the war in garrison duty in and around Nashville.

The terms of enlistment for members of the Forty-seventh Ohio, Company B, ran out in late August 1864. Many of them had not reenlisted and began the journey back to Lenawee County. Those who elected to serve another term found themselves joining Sherman on his famous March to the Sea.

Petersburg

After Grant's attack on June 15, both Union and Confederate troops settled into a siege outside Petersburg, Virginia. Soldiers in the Union army spent time catching up on news, writing home and mending uniforms. Faron Anderson recounted in a July 12 letter to his mother that he was able to acquire bread, and with his pay, he could buy honey, molasses, butter, canned fruit, condensed milk, ginger cakes, hot pies and biscuits from the sutlers (merchants who followed the army).[52]

Front line duty was risky. Sharpshooters and artillery fire were a continual threat for pickets and guards placed within sight of the enemy in the trenches. Faron Anderson's family learned how dangerous seemly quiet times in the war could be.

On July 13, Faron Anderson would be shot just above the right hip while in the forward trenches of the Second Michigan. The hospital workers believed his wound was not serious, but in the early hours of July 14, Anderson called for a friend to come be with him. Faron died shortly after.

In a letter to his parents in Tecumseh, a fellow soldier wrote:

> *He is burried* [sic] *in the 3rd Division, 9th Corp burial ground. It is on Burchards Plantation about three miles southeast of Petersburg. His grave*

The grave site of Faron Anderson in Brookside Cemetery in Tecumseh, Michigan. Anderson was twice wounded while in service and died outside the trenches in Petersburg on July 15, 1864. *Courtesy of Kara Lennard.*

is marked with his name, company and regiment with ink and for fear it will wash off in the rain I will cut it on the right side of the board.[53]

In an effort to end the deadlock, a group of Pennsylvania miners in General Burnside's Ninth Corps offered an idea to end the siege. They proposed to tunnel under Confederate fortifications and blow up the Rebel lines. Union forces could then simply waltz into the destroyed section of line and roll up Confederate forces.

Construction of the tunnel began in late June, and by the end of July the tunnel was complete. The tunnel would be packed with 320 kegs of black powder and sealed. On July 30 at 4:44 a.m., the powder exploded and the attack began.

Burnside planned for African American troops to charge directly toward the newly created hole in the Confederate lines. Union troops would attack across the front as well to keep Confederates from shifting troops to plug the hole. Initially, it appeared the plan would work. The explosion created the hole in the Rebel works and killed nearly three hundred defenders. Unharmed troops were stunned at the massive explosion, and it took nearly a quarter hour for commanders to re-form the scattered troops into a defensive force.

A ten-minute delay in the main attacking force, coupled with a lack of ladders to climb out of the newly formed crater, turned the tides on the plan. Troops poured into the hole in the ground only to find they could not climb out. As Confederate reinforcements arrived, the plan fell apart.

William Humphrey of the Second Michigan was in charge of the brigade of soldiers to the immediate left of the crater. Men from the First, Second and Twentieth Michigan attempted to check the counterattacks of the Rebels and allow for the main Union attacking force to escape. After a short time, the men were compelled to fall back.

Humphrey's performance during what became known as the "Overland Campaign" in the spring and summer of 1864 made General Grant take notice. Humphrey aptly commanded brigades at Spotsylvania, Cold Harbor and during operations at Petersburg. Grant offered command of the First Division of the Eighteenth Corps to Humphrey until he could find a suitable replacement. Rather than take the promotion and extend his term of service, Humphrey resigned on the spot.

The siege of Petersburg continued. Henry H. Daniels gave a glimpse of what siege duty was like in a letter home to J.K. Boies of Hudson. Daniels enlisted in the Second Michigan as a sergeant at the outbreak of the war. He had risen to the rank of captain of Company C, Second Michigan. Daniels participated in the ill-fated attack at the crater on the July 30. The letter would be published in the July 23 edition of the *Hudson Gazette*:

> *Our position is in a rifle pit a little south of east from Petersburg, a distant less than a mile but on account of its being settled down between the hills can only see the "steeples." The rebel line of works are about 400 yards in front of us; our pickets are about ½ way between. There is not much picket firing as there has been, but the artillery opens occasionally and makes the dust fly if nothing more. There are a great many mortars used on both sides. They are fired with so small a charge of powder that the first intimation*

we have of their evil intentions is a fluttering in the air, when a tremendous explosion. We drop the shells into their pits with great precision and we sometimes see blankets, tents and even Johnnies, taking excursions in the air.

THE EIGHTEENTH AT ATHENS

In the fall of 1864, the Eighteenth Michigan was stationed at Decatur, Georgia. In this spot, the Eighteenth was assigned to guard and provost duty. On September 24, a small detachment of the regiment (around 230 men) marched to reinforce a fort at Athens, Georgia.

Two miles from the fort, the Eighteenth was attacked by a force of Confederate cavalry, estimated to be four thousand strong, under the command of General Nathan Bedford Forrest. The Eighteenth fought the two miles to reach the fort, only to run out of ammunition and to find that the fort had already surrendered.

The party surrendered to the Confederates. The captives were sent to prison camps. Some of the men managed to escape, however. William Harrison Marshall of Ogden recalled in his diary:

A postwar photograph of members of Company C, Eighteenth Michigan Infantry. *Courtesy of Lenawee County Historical Museum.*

> *I was on the front skirmish line all the while until about a minute before the skirmish line was captured. And by running a desperate chance for my life I succeeded in reaching a thicket where I concealed myself from the Rebels for 5 hours.*[54]

The men who were captured were sent to one of two camps: Andersonville in Georgia or Cahaba Prison (known as Castle Morgan) not far from Selma, Alabama. Andersonville held nearly forty thousand prisoners, and about thirteen thousand of them would die of starvation and disease. Cahaba was a smaller camp, housing only three thousand prisoners along the bank of the Cahaba River.

Many men of the Eighteenth who were captured at Athens survived the harrowing experience of prison camps. Released in April 1865, the survivors faced a greater challenge on the Mississippi River on their way home.

Eleventh Michigan Cavalry

The unit that would become the Eleventh Michigan Cavalry began recruiting in the fall of 1863. Enlistment offices opened in Clinton and Hudson, enticing a number of Lenawee County men to join the cavalry. By December 1863, the unit was ready to leave the state and numbered nearly one thousand men.

In early 1864, the Eleventh Cavalry patrolled the countryside of Kentucky in an effort to keep lawlessness in check. In June, the Federal horsemen battled Confederate cavalry and partisan rangers under the command of John Hunt Morgan in what would be his last raid in Kentucky. On June 12, 1864, Rebel forces, under Morgan, faced off the Eleventh Michigan, Federal infantry and Ohio cavalry. Outnumbered nearly 2 to 1 and low on ammunition, the Confederate horsemen fled Cynthiana, Kentucky, in haste. Morgan's command was wrecked; of the nearly 1,200 men who entered the battle, only 200 escaped into western Virginia.

In the fall of 1864, members of the Eleventh Michigan Cavalry participated in a coordinated raid to capture and destroy the salt mines of western Virginia. Under the command of General Stephen G. Burnbridge, the Eleventh made its way to Saltville, Virginia. The mines were vital to the Confederate cause, as the salt allowed for meats to be cured and sent to the field. In October, Federal forces made their move.

Left: Lieutenant William Baker Thompson of Hudson. Thompson enlisted in the Eleventh Michigan Cavalry and, at war's end, transferred to the Eighth Michigan Cavalry. *Courtesy of W.G. Thompson House Museum.*

Below: The field desk of William Baker Thompson, who served the Eleventh Michigan as quartermaster beginning in June 1865. *Courtesy of Hudson Museum.*

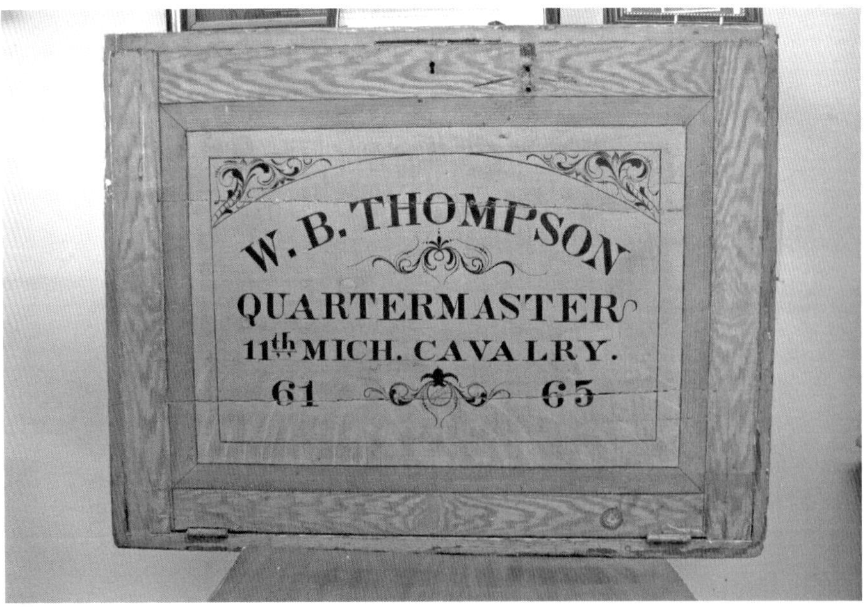

The Federal horsemen found the area heavily defended by Confederate forces. The Eleventh participated in several skirmishes as the Union command attempted to formulate an attack plan. Finally, on October 2, General Burnbridge ordered a charge on the fortifications. The Eleventh and a unit of African American cavalry troops attacked. The Eleventh lost eighty-six men killed, wounded or missing in a fight where they were nearly surrounded. The African American troops fared far worse. In the aftermath of the attack, Confederate troops massacred the wounded black soldiers.

The Eleventh regrouped after the ill-fated attack and participated in a lightning-quick raid into North Carolina in November. In December, the unit returned to Saltville, Virginia, to capture the salt mines. This time, the attack worked. The Eleventh Michigan participated in the destruction of over two thousand kettles used for evaporating salt and spoiled the salt wells by pouring solid shot and railroad iron down the wells.

Along with the destruction of the saltworks, the men of the Eleventh captured two arsenals filled with munitions and cannons, destroyed several storehouses used for provisions and captured five locomotives with cars. The losses were deeply felt by the Confederate armies in Petersburg and North Carolina, as the Eleventh's raid entered areas untouched by war up to this point.

Wartime Election

In October, newspapers began to mix in political news as the presidential election crept closer. George B. McClellan, known affectionately as "Little Mac" by the soldiers who loved him, ran for president as the Democrat Party candidate. Abraham Lincoln faced the difficult task of winning reelection in a nation growing weary of war. The October 29 edition of the *Hudson Gazette* published two letters, one in support of McClellan, while the other called for Lincoln to be elected. The editor published them under the headings of "Copperhead" and "Abolition."

The letter for McClellan cited food shortages for the men serving in the field, the stalemate on the battlefield and the lack of prompt payment to the soldiers. He wrote, "How is old Abe's prospectus up North? I tell you if they are half as gloomy as they are here, his chance of re-election is slim. . . . I hope the people of the US will elect a man of more capability." In another section, he wrote, "If [those at home] had gone through a campaign of 3 years such as I have, perhaps it would cool their love of niggers some."

The opposing viewpoint offered by another soldier in the field was short and to the point:

> *You say the man or party that will clean up the war the quickest is the one. I don't want this war to close until we can close it with honor to Northern arms; and I also want slavery to become extinct and blotted out forever, and then I will be satisfied to come home and stay. I have seen too much blood shed to see it closed in any other way. I may have children myself, and I don't want them in a country where slavery exists. It is a cure to any nation, and now the irons are hot, let us cool them to suit ourselves.*

Thanks to Sherman's victory in Atlanta, coupled with the antislavery vote, Lincoln handily won a second term to carry on the war effort.

6

1865: End of Hostilities

As the calendar turned to 1865, there was an air of optimism in the newspaper reports in Lenawee County. While Grant had Lee's forces pinned down at Petersburg, Virginia, other Federal forces were enjoying success in the field. General William T. Sherman marched from Atlanta to Savannah, arriving in that city on December 21, 1864. The Confederate Army of Tennessee ceased to exist after the Franklin/Nashville campaign of November and December 1864. Hood's Rebels were smashed in mid-December outside Nashville, Tennessee, and after their retreat to northern Alabama, the army lost all organization.

Reports and editorials now focused on the growing temperance movement in Lenawee County, as well as other events in the county. A February 9, 1865 article in the *Tecumseh Herald* noted the construction of a new Masonic Hall in Adrian at an estimated cost of $40,000 to $50,000. The construction of the Masonic Hall was started as another project, the Union Opera Hall, made news for nearing completion.

The feeling that the end of the war was near spurred renewed drives for the Sanitary Commission. Reports on the successful fundraising drives in Hudson and Adrian led to new efforts in Tecumseh. The *Tecumseh Herald* reported on February 9: "Young people of this place . . . organized a society for the purpose of giving entertainment consisting of dialogues, tableaux, orations and music to be given sometime next week." The funds would be given to the Ladies' Aid Society.

A push to fill the congressional quotas continued in the county. Residents of towns, villages and townships hoped to raise funds or find enlistees so that their hometowns would be spared in the March draft. Ridgeway provides an example of the length the residents would go to for this effort.

Ridgeway created a permanent military organization dedicated to finding enlistees or substitutes to fill that township's quota. The residents elected a board that would be authorized to take donations and negotiate with individuals to fill enlistment slots. By the end of February, the organization had raised nearly $2,000 and found two men willing to

George B. Swift enlisted in Company D, Eleventh Michigan Cavalry, in September 1863. Swift rose to the rank of corporal before his discharge in October 1865, when he returned to Hudson. *Courtesy of Hudson Museum.*

enlist. Unfortunately for the board, it needed to fill twelve more slots, and the draft came again in March.

The grind of war continued for the men in the field. As Rebel armies dissolved, many of the Confederates took to guerrilla warfare. A member of the Eleventh Michigan Cavalry gives a glimpse of the type of fighting this entailed when he wrote to the *Tecumseh Herald* (published on February 23, 1865):

> *The depredations of guerrillas and horse thieves continue to be a great annoyance to the people, especially those who are known to be loyal. No section of the country seems to be sacred from their visitations. They prowled about mostly at night and we are unable to capture but few of them from the fact that at the approach of any armed detachment of soldiers, they instantly dissolve their organization and each man betakes himself to his mountain recess . . .*

End of the War

On March 25, Confederate troops at Petersburg made a desperate attack near a Union position known as Fort Stedman. The attack was an attempt to break the siege and gain much-needed supplies by targeting the Union supply hub of City Point. Union forces that opposed the Rebels in the predawn attack included men from the Second and Seventeenth Michigan.

Captain John Boughton, who commanded the Second Michigan, wrote the following about the attack: "A crowd of men came running down the trench. Supposing they were of one of our regiments, and running away from the enemy, I stepped out and ordered them to halt, saying that it was useless to run away." Just at that moment, a man put a hand on his shoulder and asked the captain to go with him. Boughton had been captured by Rebels. He ordered his men to fire, disrupting the attack and allowing members of the Second Michigan to escape the situation.[55]

The Seventeenth Michigan Infantry was one of the Federal units that participated in the counterattack as dawn broke. Slowly, Union infantry and artillery checked the Confederate attack and forced them back to their original position. The attack would be the last attack of the Rebel Army of Northern Virginia.

Charles Cleveland recorded in his diary the events of March 25: "A battle was recently fought between a portion of our army under Grant and the rebels under Lee, in which our forces were successful—The rebellion is short lived."[56] He followed up with: "Everyone, whether copperhead or not, now fully believes that the end of the rebellion is nigh, and in a short time, slavery will forever cease on this continent."[57]

On April 2, Union forces broke through the Confederate defenses at Petersburg. The 292-day siege at Petersburg was over. Just one week later, on Sunday, April 9, 1865, Lee would surrender the Rebel army to Grant at Appomattox Court House. The war was over!

News of the end of the hostilities were reasons for joyous celebration. The *Tecumseh Herald* reported the events in the April 13 edition:

> *We venture to say that the news which reached our quiet village by the Monday morning train from Jackson found no more hearty welcome in the broad land than right here. It was the full tidings of Lee's surrender to our invincible Grant. . . . The offices, shops, school rooms and studies had been opened for the week's work when suddenly church bells began to peel out the notes of victory. The steam whistles joined the chorus. Men dropped their implements of labor, the pen was laid aside, the law book thrown upon the shelf, the prescription half made out was thrust into the hands of the druggist, the merchant pushed his goods out of the way, told his customers to call again, and the next moment an eager crowd gathering the welcome news from the Post Office bulletin.*

The citizens of Tecumseh were treated to impromptu speeches by local leaders, and there was singing of "John Brown's Body" and "The Star-Spangled Banner" to mark the occasion.

Charles Cleveland recorded the news of Lee's surrender in his April 10 diary entry:

> *The glorious news of Lee's surrender was received this morning. At 12 o'clock AM all the bells of the city commenced ringing. The city was wild with joy. All kinds of noises were made. In the evening—illuminations, bonfires, torchlight processions all took place.*

On April 11, Cleveland wrote:

> *This city never saw such grand rejoicing as took place yesterday. Everybody let loose and "went it big." The streets were literally filled with fireballs, rockets and all manners of pyrotechnics. I never shall forget this celebration. All quiet today.*

When Confederate general Joseph Johnson learned of Lee's surrender, he began negotiations with General William Tecumseh Sherman. Three separate negotiation meetings finally led to the surrender of the remaining Confederate forces in the field. With that, the Civil War was over.

Lincoln Assassinated

On the evening of April 14, Abraham Lincoln attended a play, *Our American Cousin*, at Ford's Theatre in Washington, D.C. Shortly after the intermission, John Wilkes Booth entered the president's box and shot Lincoln. Jumping to the stage, Booth escaped.

In other parts of Washington, D.C., allies of Booth attempted to assassinate Lincoln's vice president and secretary of state. George Atzerodt was ordered to kill Vice President Andrew Johnson; however, Atzerodt imbibed too much alcohol and opted not to commit the act. Lewis Powell, with the assistance of David Herold, was tasked with killing Secretary of State William Seward. Powell did manage to enter Seward's home and inflict stab wounds to the secretary of state. During the attack, Herold fled the scene, and Powell was forced to roam the unfamiliar streets of Washington in an attempt to escape.

The news of the assassination reached Adrian on April 15. Charles Cleveland recorded:

> *Our community was terribly shocked this morning by the telegraphic announcement that Abraham Lincoln, President of the US was last night at 9 o'clock shot in a theatre in Washington, and that he died at 22 minutes past 7 o'clock this morning. Nor could we believe it until dispatch after dispatch confirmed it. Business was almost entirely suspended, bells were tolled, and the city hung in deep mourning. All seemed to share in the sorrow. Such universal, heartfelt mourning was never before witnessed in this land. The great, good Abraham Lincoln assassinated! and too, just now, after having passed such a terrible war as this has been, and when peace, a great glorious one, was at hand. Words cannot express the anguish of the nation—God save us!*

The Booth conspirators would be rounded up shortly after the plot. Powell was found on April 17 at the inn of Mary Surratt. Both were arrested. Atzerodt would be tracked to a family member's house on April 20. Booth would be located and fatally shot on April 26, 1865.

On May 1, 1865, the military trial of the four conspirators, plus four accused of assisting the conspirators, started. The conspirators were held at Washington, D.C. Arsenal. Richard A. Watts, the Adrian College student who joined the First Michigan and, later, the Seventeenth Michigan, was appointed to be in charge of communication between the prison and the War Department.

Watts was wounded in action during the April 2 attack on Petersburg. He was in Lenawee County nursing his wounds when the news of Lincoln's death reached Lenawee County. Returning to Washington on April 25, he took on his new responsibility.

Watts wrote a detailed reminiscence of his participation in the events for *Michigan History* magazine. The seven-week trial called 366 witnesses. In the end, all 8 accused were found guilty on June 30. Only Powell, Atzerodt, Suratt and Herold were ordered to die by hanging for their actions on July 7. The other 4 members accused of assisting the conspirators were sentenced to other forms of punishment. Watts recalled their execution:

> *Between one and two o'clock of that day, July 7th, Mrs. Surratt, Herold, Atzerodt and Payne were removed from their cells and escorted by a soldier on each side to the gallows standing in the open area inside of the high brick wall. Mrs. Surratt was accompanied by two Catholic priests, each carrying a crucifix and breviary, and uttering a prayer which Mrs. Surratt seemed to be repeating. This scene was most solemn and affecting. Each of the others was also attended by a clergyman.*
>
> *The four were assisted to ascend the steps leading up to the gallows platform and seated in chairs. Major General Hartranft and staff, in full dress uniform, passed up onto the platform, and the General at once in a low quiet tone read the sentences. While reading, the general's hat was removed and, the sun being excessively hot, the writer of this narrative held an umbrella over him.*
>
> *The ropes, fastened to a cross beam above, dangled in front of each. The noose was quickly adjusted upon each by a secret service officer and they were required to rise and step forward upon the traps, Mrs. Surratt and Payne upon one, Herold and Atzerodt upon the other. The traps were held in position by heavy braces beneath. Capt. Rath gave a signal, the two braces were knocked from under by a heavy beam swung by two soldiers, and the four simultaneously dropped to death and eternity.*
>
> *After thirty minutes each was examined by Surgeon Porter, pronounced dead, taken down and placed in separate boxes. To avoid any mistake in identification in the future, I wrote the name of each upon a slip of paper, sealed it up in a small bottle, and placed it in each respective box.*

Richard A. Watts is the gentleman holding the umbrella in the in the center of this image showing the execution of the Lincoln conspirators. *Courtesy of the Library of Congress.*

> *A detail of soldiers at once closed the covers and buried them in separate graves just inside the prison wall.*
>
> *Within a day or two the other four, Arnold, Spangler, O'Laughlin and Dr. Mudd, were placed upon a man of war and taken under charge of Col. Dodd to the military prison at Dry Tortugas.*
>
> *The remains of Booth had been buried underneath one of the prison cells the night before our occupying the prison.*[58]

Capture of Confederate President Jefferson Davis

When Richmond fell on April 2, the Confederate government packed up to flee to the Deep South. Taking the train to Danville, Virginia, Davis and his cabinet moved overland by horse to Charlotte, North Carolina, and eventually on to Abbeville, South Carolina. As the Rebel government made its way into Georgia, Federal troops were on the lookout for the band.

One of the groups tracking Davis and his cabinet were members of the Fourth Michigan Cavalry. The Fourth Cavalry mustered in in August 1862 and included several enlistees from Lenawee County, including Richard B. Robbins of Adrian. Robbins enlisted as captain of Company F and rose to the rank of major before being wounded. He would be discharged as a brevetted lieutenant colonel. The unit fought in the western theater in various actions, including Stones River, Chickamauga and Atlanta.

The Fourth Cavalry was alerted on April 21 that there was a possibility that Davis could be heading its way. On the morning of May 7, the sound of bugle calls filled camp. The men were ordered to mount up, as the unit would be heading out on patrol. Julian Dickinson recalled the moment after the war:

> *Though the purpose of the expedition had not been disclosed to any of our troopers, it became apparent before the termination of the first day's march, that many of them had grasped some knowledge of its purpose; it created some excitement among the men and occasioned remarks relative to the object of our pursuit, which threatened to render the success of the expedition problematical. On the evening of the seventh we went into bivouac for the night on a beautiful plantation near Hawkinsville. Our headquarters occupied the porch of the plantation dwelling, a fortunate situation for us, for a thunderstorm broke over us that night, the lightning spreading havoc in the camp.*[59]

On May 8, the horsemen received word that a large train of ambulances and wagons was on the road ahead, traveling in the direction of Irwinville, Georgia. Later in the day, the Fourth Cavalry questioned an African American gentleman who was working on a broken-down wagon. He reported assisting a large body of gentlemen ford a river. The men paid in gold coins and were riding "fine horses."

The horsemen speculated that this group must have been part of Davis's traveling party. The command of the Fourth Michigan Cavalry detached 128 men and 7 officers to probe out from the main body. One of the members of the advanced guard was a man from the Macon area, William Crittenden.

The Fourth reached Irwinville after dark. The men proceeded to wake residents, inquiring about wagon trains and riders. The residents claimed to have known nothing about the party, and then the horsemen finally got a break. An African American man gave the needed information:

> *He stated there had been several mounted men to the house ring the afternoon, from a camp near the village, to purchase forage and provisions, and the camp lay about a mile and a half out on the Abbeville road. Placing the freedman in advance for guide, and directing the utmost silence to be preserved in the column, we moved out on the Abbeville road. The night was rather dark, but clear and very quiet. We marched the distance of about a mile when we halted and made the necessary arrangements for the capture of the camp when light was deemed sufficient to enable us to discern its situation.*[60]

On the morning of the tenth, the Fourth Michigan Cavalry descended on the encampment. A man dressed in women's clothing attempted to flee. It was Jefferson Davis. The horsemen had their man.

Sultana

After the fall of the Confederacy, the prisoners of war held in Andersonville and other Southern prison camps were free. The United States War Department wanted to get the men back to their homes as quickly as possible and offered steamboat captains five dollars per enlisted man and ten dollars per officer to transport the POWs back north. At Vicksburg, Mississippi, the Federal government gathered ex-prisoners from Andersonville and Cahaba for transport home.

The *Sultana* docked in Vicksburg on April 23 for repairs to the boiler and to take on passengers. The ship was legally licensed to carry 376 passengers. More than 2,000 men boarded the steamer for the trip north. On the evening of April 24, the *Sultana* left the dock for the trip north.

The boat struggled up the Mississippi, swollen from spring rains. On April 26, the *Sultana* docked in Memphis, Tennessee, to take on coal and offload 120 tons of sugar. At 2:00 a.m. on April 27, the boiler blew up. Passengers were flung into the raging river. The boat caught fire and began to sink.

Passengers were forced to make decisions about what to do to survive. Many of the men were weak from their ordeal of being prisoners of war and simply slid under the surface of the water and died. Others clung to scraps of wood floating to the safety of the shore.

Over forty men from Lenawee County were on board. Most had served in the Eighteenth Michigan Infantry and were captured outside

Above: On April 26, 1865, the *Sultana* docked at Helena, Arkansas, to take on supplies and more men. The grossly overloaded boat sank in the worst maritime disaster in American history. *Courtesy of the Library of Congress.*

Left: The grave site of the Rowley brothers, Orson and Warren, who perished on the *Sultana*. Both brothers served in the Eighteenth Michigan Infantry. *Courtesy of Kara Lennard.*

Decatur, Alabama. Henry Koon of Hudson was one of the men aboard the boat. He recounted:

> *From here we were removed on board the steamer* Sultana, *and started up the river on our way to Camp Chase, Ohio. On the morning of the 27th of April, as we all know, the ill-fated steamer was blown up, and finally the fire compelled me to jump off. After I was in the water I managed to get hold of a couple sticks of wood that were floating in the water, and secured one under each arm, thus buoyed myself up (not being able to swim at all), until I had floated down the stream, I judge, about 5 or 6 miles, when I was picked up by a steamer after sunrise, between six and seven o'clock, I think, I can not* [sic] *state exact time. I think I was forced into the water about 3 o'clock a.m.*[61]

William Thayer, a member of Company B of the Eighteenth Michigan from Adrian, wrote:

> *I was lying in the alley way of the second deck when the boat blew up. I stayed on the boat until I saw two scantlings tied together with a pair of suspenders, I thought they would help me along and they did, for I floated down the river for about six miles and then neared the shore. I climbed a tree and tied myself there with my shirt, and about two o'clock P.M. I was picked up.*[62]

A memoir by Walter G. Porter of Fairfield went into great detail on the events leading up to the explosion and the aftermath. Porter reported getting off the boat in Memphis to tour the city while the steamer took on coal. When he returned, he was forced to find a new location to sleep, eventually sleeping near the staircase with his feet hanging over the steps.

When the explosion rocked the boat, Porter thought that one of the decks had collapsed from the overcrowding. Once he knew the boat was going down, Porter stripped off his clothes to make a floatation device. Jumping from the boat, the clothing float was lost. Porter went on:

> *The most that I was afraid of was that some drowning man would catch hold of me. While making for shore I passed four men astride of something, using their hands for oars, and one of them gave the orders so that they would work together. When I got to land, or where the land is most of the time, I found that it was covered with water. The trees were quite dense,*

> *and out in the woods a few rods I found a large tree that was floating in the water, climbed upon it and called to some others that were trying to find a place to get out of the water. Some came and got on the log with me, and several got another log near by. I had to rub myself considerably to keep warm, as I did not have any clothing on. Remained there about four or five hours, when a boat came along and picked me up. When I got on to the boat they gave me a sheet to wrap around me.*

An estimated 1,800 people perished in the little-known naval disaster, including over 30 from Lenawee County. The full extent of the disaster may never be fully known, as the record of passengers was spotty and the news of the sinking was overshadowed by the events surrounding the assassination of Abraham Lincoln.

RECOGNITION OF SACRIFICE

On May 25, 1865, a letter to the editor of the *Tecumseh Herald* appeared in print. The author called for a monument to the sacrifices of those who fell in the war to defend the Union. A follow-up letter on May 31 stated, "Let us go to work at once to prepare a suitable monument to their memory. Let the monument be located in a conspicuous place in our beautiful village cemetery."

The Tecumseh area was a natural choice for the first calls for the erection of a monument. There were 119 men killed from Tecumseh, Macon, Ridgeway, Raisin and Franklin. At a picnic celebrating the Fourth of July, nearly $900 was raised toward a fitting structure. Finally, in 1882, the monument went up in Military Square. In 1928, the monument was relocated to Brookside Cemetery.

Why did it take seventeen years for the Tecumseh monument to finally go up? The answer partially lies in an October 13, 1865 plea for a meeting at the Bidwell Hall in Adrian. Orsamus Lamb and C.E. Weaver called for a countywide convention of appointed citizens for the purpose of forming a committee to explore the erection of a soldiers' monument for all Lenawee County Civil War veterans.

The following article ran in local papers: "Already in many parts of the County funds have been raised for this object but as yet there is no general plan of action and it is for the purpose of concentrating all efforts upon some one plan, that this convention is called."

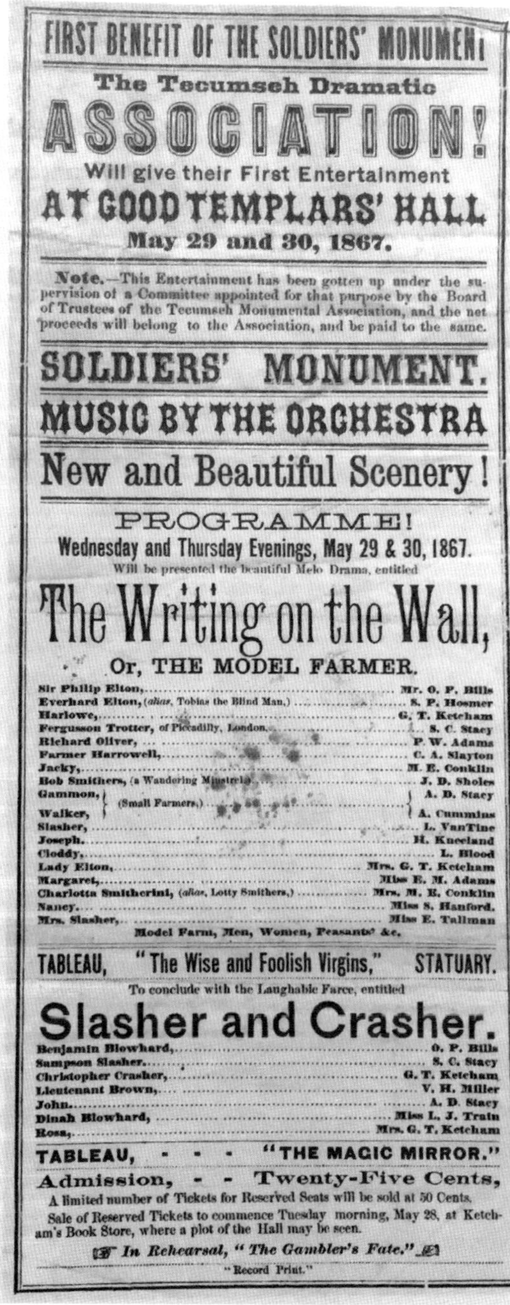

FIRST BENEFIT OF THE SOLDIERS' MONUMENT

The Tecumseh Dramatic

ASSOCIATION!

Will give their First Entertainment

AT GOOD TEMPLARS' HALL

May 29 and 30, 1867.

Note.—This Entertainment has been gotten up under the supervision of a Committee appointed for that purpose by the Board of Trustees of the Tecumseh Monumental Association, and the net proceeds will belong to the Association, and be paid to the same.

SOLDIERS' MONUMENT.

MUSIC BY THE ORCHESTRA

New and Beautiful Scenery!

PROGRAMME!

Wednesday and Thursday Evenings, May 29 & 30, 1867.

Will be presented the beautiful Melo Drama, entitled

The Writing on the Wall,

Or, THE MODEL FARMER.

Sir Philip Elton, ... Mr. O. P. Bills
Everhard Elton, (*alias*, Tobias the Blind Man,) .... S. P. Hosmer
Harlowe, ... G. T. Ketcham
Fergusson Trotter, of Piccadilly, London, ... S. C. Stacy
Richard Oliver, ... P. W. Adams
Farmer Harrowell, ... C. A. Slayton
Jacky, ... M. E. Conklin
Bob Smithers, (a Wandering Minstrel,) .... J. D. Sholes
Gammon, } (Small Farmers,) .... { A. D. Stacy
Walker, } .... { A. Cummins
Slasher, ... L. VanTine
Joseph, ... H. Kneeland
Cloddy, ... L. Blood
Lady Elton, ... Mrs. G. T. Ketcham
Margaret, ... Miss E. M. Adams
Charlotta Smitherini, (*alias*, Lotty Smithers,) .... Mrs. M. E. Conklin
Nancy, ... Miss S. Hanford.
Mrs. Slasher, ... Miss E. Tallman

Model Farm, Men, Women, Peasants' &c.

TABLEAU, "The Wise and Foolish Virgins," STATUARY.

To conclude with the Laughable Farce, entitled

Slasher and Crasher.

Benjamin Blowhard, ... O. P. Bills
Sampson Slasher, ... S. C. Stacy
Christopher Crasher, ... G. T. Ketcham
Lieutenant Brown, ... V. H. Miller
John, ... A. D. Stacy
Dinah Blowhard, ... Miss L. J. Train
Rosa, ... Mrs. G. T. Ketcham

TABLEAU, - - - "THE MAGIC MIRROR."

Admission, - - Twenty-Five Cents,

A limited number of Tickets for Reserved Seats will be sold at 50 Cents.

Sale of Reserved Tickets to commence Tuesday morning, May 28, at Ketcham's Book Store, where a plot of the Hall may be seen.

In Rehearsal, "The Gambler's Fate."

"Record Print."

A broadside advertising the first fundraiser for the Tecumseh Civil War Monument. Fund mismanagement led to a delay in erecting the memorial to those who served. *Courtesy of Clara Waldron Historical Room, Tecumseh District Library.*

A postcard showing the original site of the Tecumseh monument in Military Square, where local troops trained to go off to war. *Courtesy of Clara Waldron Historical room, Tecumseh District Library.*

On November 4, 1865, the committee met. The delegates quickly agreed that Adrian's pledge to donate one-fourth of the total cost was fair and should be accepted. Next, officers were elected: Henry Hart of Adrian became chair, with John K. Boies (Hudson), Gideon D. Perry (Franklin Township), J.S. Hodges (Ogden Township), G.W. Teachout (Rome Township) and E.L. Clark (Adrian) as vice presidents. Norman Geddes served as the group's secretary, while W.H. Stone became treasurer. Each city and township outside Adrian was granted a seat for a director, while one director would be appointed for each of the four wards for the city of Adrian.

The officers and directors were granted the full power and authority of the convention to "fix and agree upon the design, plans and specifications for a County Soldier's Monument."[63] In addition, the officers could fundraise for the monument, as well as replace any vacancies on the committee. The last action of the committee was to approve a proposal by W.H. Cleveland that called for the name of every soldier from Lenawee County "deceased while in the service of his country" to be engraved on the monument.

December 1865 and January 1866 passed with little mention of the County Monument Association in the local newspapers. Through a lack of action, local entities began fundraising for a monument to be located in their area. Franklin Township was one such locale.

In early 1866, Andrew J. Hunter, the appointee to serve on the County Monument Association, began to raise funds in Franklin Township for the purpose of the creation of a local monument. P.C. Mills, Samuel Wilson and D.W. Mapes soon joined in the fundraising efforts. The men quickly agreed that any donation would be accepted, but soldiers were allowed to donate only one dollar. The men felt that veterans of the Union had done enough for the area.

Lydia Smith had the honor of donating the first fifty dollars to the Franklin Monument Fund. Mrs. Smith sent three sons off to serve, with only one returning. John and Allen C. Smith served in the Ninth Michigan Cavalry. Allen received fatal wounds in action near Waynesboro, Georgia. John contracted the measles in training camp at Grand Rapids, Michigan, in March 1864. Only William survived the war, enlisting in the Eighteenth Michigan and returning home in June 1865.

In three months, the citizens of Franklin secured the needed funds. The *Adrian Weekly Times* reported that the monument was in the process of being carved at the shop of Knight, Harrison and Company of Adrian. In May, the following ad appeared:

> *The citizens of Franklin are to put on the top stone of their Soldiers' Monument on the coming 4th, and in connection therewith intend to celebrate the day. The order of exercises at the Monument will consist of Prayer, singing, speaking and firing of cannon. The procession will then be formed, and march, under the charge of the Marshal, and with music, to an appropriate place to listen to an oration and other speaking, and partake of a picnic dinner.*

The dedication of the Franklin Township Civil War monument was well attended, as estimates counted nearly 1,400 people. Starting at the Presbyterian church, the crowd gathered to listen to the Reverend Dr. Lee deliver an eloquent speech. From the church, the crowd marched to A. Camburn's home to listen to the main speaker for the day, Charles Croswell. His forty-five-minute speech covered the history of warfare and strife but closed with the following:

> *You have erected and consecrated a monument to the memory of the noble sons of Franklin who perished in the war. As I rode along this morning and saw your fields of waving grain, your pleasant homesteads and beautiful surroundings, I felt how deep a debt you owed to those patriots. You owe it to them that your fields have not been laid waste, your homes burned and the country devastated. Their memory should be ever cherished. And see to*

On July 6, 2006, the community of Franklin Township came together to rededicate the restored Civil War monument located in the cemetery. The elements eroded the soft sandstone, and a tornado removed the finial from the staff of the monument. *Courtesy of Hudson Museum.*

> *it that no tender child of any of these brave ones suffer. . . . Remember that as you honor the memory of these men and succor their children, so you honor yourselves.*[64]

Those in attendance gathered in a nearby grove of trees for a picnic. Several toasts were made, songs were sung and food was consumed.

In 1870, the City of Adrian finally erected a monument to honor the men from the city who died during the Civil War. Benjamin Latrobe created the monument at a cost of $10,000. The memorial features a column from the

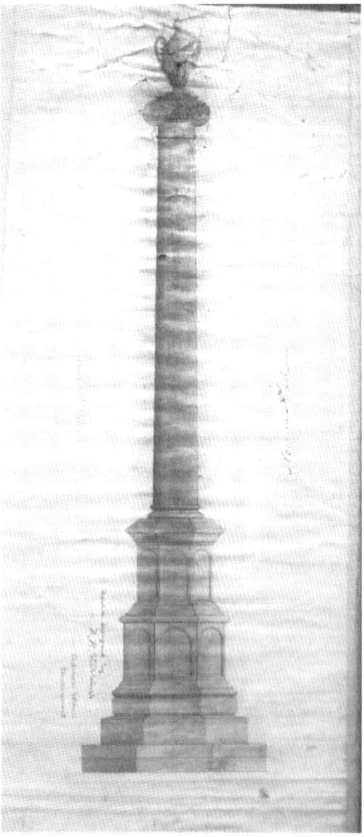

Left: Blueprint plans for the Adrian soldiers' and sailors' monument located in Memorial Park. The column came from the former Bank of Pennsylvania building in Philadelphia. *Courtesy of Lenawee County Historical Museum.*

Right: A photo postcard of the Adrian soldiers' and sailors' monument decorated for Memorial Day, circa 1900. *Courtesy of Lenawee County Historical Museum.*

former Bank of Pennsylvania building in Philadelphia. The bank was torn down in 1868, and Congress sold the column to the city for the memorial.

The Adrian monument was unveiled on July 4, 1870. The memorial lists the names of eighty-four men who died in service to the nation. On the base is the inscription: "Erected by citizens of Adrian in memory of our fallen soldiers. By such as these was our Union saved in the great struggle of 1861–1865."

In the Lime Creek Cemetery stands a carved obelisk to the memory of thirty-three men from the Medina Township area. The monument is somewhat of a mystery, as there is no reference to the date of the erection or just why or how the thirty-three men came to be memorialized on the marker. One local historian believes that the monument was placed there by the family and friends of the men on the marker so that their sacrifice would not be forgotten.[65]

7

Postwar Lenawee

GAR

After the war, returning soldiers sought ways to maintain contact with their comrades. On April 6, 1866, Benjamin F. Stephenson founded the Grand Army of the Republic (GAR). Membership was limited to honorably

A group photograph of GAR post number 45 standing on the Lenawee County Courthouse steps, circa 1890. *Courtesy of Lenawee County Historical Museum.*

discharged veterans of the Union army, navy, marine corps or revenue cutter service who had served between April 12, 1861, and April 9, 1865.

The organization, known by its initials GAR, was a national one. Locally, groups of soldiers formed posts. Posts became part of a larger group covering a region known as a department. The organization was primarily a fraternal organization but later worked actively for veterans' relief and pension issues.

Lenawee County had twelve GAR posts that served the needs of the veterans. For the most part, the GAR posts were named after a local man (or men) who had given his life to the cause of the Union. There were two exceptions: Addison post (post 227, operated from 1884 to 1902), which was never named, and the Palmyra post, which was named after a veteran who died at the time the post opened.

Adrian post number 45 (1882 to 1945): named for Dwight D. Woodbury, colonel of the Fourth Michigan Infantry, who was killed in action at Malvern Hill on July 1, 1862.

Blissfield post number 43 (1882 to 1930): named for Patrick Scott, member of the Twenty-seventh Michigan Infantry, who died as a prisoner of war after being captured at Petersburg, Virginia.

Britton post number 222 (1884 to 1901): named for James Eaton, a corporal in the Thirteenth Michigan Infantry, who was killed in action at Chickamauga on September 20, 1863.

Clayton post number 358 (1886 to 1922): named for the Rowley brothers, Perry, Orson and Warren, all members of the Eighteenth Michigan Infantry. Perry died of disease at Decatur, Alabama, on October 2, 1864. Orson and Warren died in the *Sultana* disaster on April 27, 1865.

Deerfield post number 12 (1880 to 1925): named for a father and son, Richard and George Ryder. Richard Ryder was a first sergeant in the Fifteenth Michigan Infantry who was killed in action at Shiloh on April 6, 1862. George Ryder was killed in action at Atlanta, Georgia, on July 22, 1864.

Hudson post number 110 (1883 to 1928): named for Samuel DeGolyer, a captain in the Fourth Michigan and later captain of a battery of horse artillery, who died of wounds received at Vicksburg.

Jasper post number 311 (1885 to 1886): named for Miles Stout of the Twelfth Michigan Infantry who died of an accidental gunshot wound on October 28, 1864.

Morenci post number 33 (dates unknown): named for Myron Baker, a lieutenant colonel of the Forty-seventh Indiana Infantry, who was killed in action at Atlanta, Georgia, on August 4, 1864.

Albert Boies (third from left) with bandmates, taken around 1900. Boies served in three wars. He enlisted in the Spanish-American War and World War I, both times guarding the homefront. *Courtesy of Hudson Museum.*

Tecumseh GAR post number 140 members posing for a photo at Brookside Cemetery prior to 1900. *Courtesy of Lenawee County Historical Museum.*

Ogden post number 25 (1881 to 1943): named for David Becker, a first sergeant in the Sixty-seventh Ohio Infantry, who was killed in action at Kernstown, Virginia, on August 4, 1864.

Palmyra post number 360 (1886 to 1912): named for Chester Corbett of the Eighteenth Michigan Infantry. Mr. Corbett died in 1886.

Tecumseh post number 140 (1883 to 1930): named for Jeptha Beers, first lieutenant in the Fourth Michigan Infantry, who was killed in action at Gaines Mills, Virginia, on May 27, 1862.

SOCIAL REFORMS

The participants in the antislavery and Underground Railroad movement, which began in the early 1800s and reached its zenith with the issuance of the Emancipation Proclamation and passage of the Thirteenth Amendment, sought new social problems to turn their efforts toward. Issues of alcohol and orphaned young women gained the attention of residents in Lenawee County in the years after the Civil War.

The temperance movement in America dated to the 1820s. Prior to the Civil War, the "Second Great Awakening" of the Protestant religion in the "burnt-over" region of western New York spread temperance into the Midwest. The newfound interest in religion commanded followers to focus on social issues deemed to be anti-Christian—such as slavery. Alcohol became a target during this time. The popularity and importance of the antislavery movement led to the temperance movement taking a backseat.

After the war, social reformers and religious followers found alcoholism to be a growing issue in America. The return of soldiers who imbibed too much whiskey could not be ignored. In 1874, a new group, the Woman's Christian Temperance Union (WCTU), gave life to a new movement in Oberlin, Ohio.

The movement quickly spread to Adrian, and by March 1874, the Woman's Christian Temperance Union had formed in Michigan. On March 10, the group organized a rally to be held at the Croswell Opera House. The meeting was for the organization of a local chapter. The keynote speaker was Laura Haviland, who would be voted president of the Lenawee County chapter. Over 1,600 people jammed into the Croswell and overflowed into the Presbyterian church.

Over the next two decades, the WCTU worked through various avenues to bring an end to the sale and consumption of alcohol locally. Some members took to sit-ins at local establishments, like saloons. Large groups of ladies

A statue of Laura Haviland situated in front of Adrian City Hall, circa 1960. The statue with water fountain was placed by members of the local chapter Woman's Christian Temperance Union in honor of Haviland's antislavery and temperance work. *Courtesy of Lenawee County Historical Museum.*

would gather, fill the property and begin praying in an attempt to publicly shame those who imbibed.

Other members worked to persuade local, state and national leaders that laws should be enacted to limit or ban alcohol. Similar to the antislavery campaign a few decades earlier, WCTU supporters backed "dry candidates" for office to enact needed legislation. Eventually, this led to the ratification of the Eighteenth Amendment in the 1920s.

The other major social cause for which local reformers worked was the cause of orphaned and troubled young women. In post–Civil War Michigan, there were not only troubled youth who came from broken homes, but also there were several orphans who had lost fathers to the war. In the late 1870s, the state legislature worked to find a way to fix the growing problem.

Finally, in 1879, the Michigan legislature passed a resolution that created a State Industrial Home for Girls. The resolution allowed for the governor of the state to select a place for the new educational campus. The governor, Charles Croswell, put out a call for proposals for towns that might be interested in having the institution in their areas.

The City of Adrian managed to find a donation of land just north of town for the campus, as well as a cash donation for the building of facilities to house the staff and young ladies. Laura Haviland headed up the local committee that made a presentation to the State Board of Control, which included William Waldby of Adrian. Adrian was selected almost immediately.

The site consisted of forty acres of land and initially six cottages. The cottages were erected for the education and housing of girls from the ages of ten to nineteen. The institution came into being when the first cottage neared completion in August 1881.

The institution worked to educate the young women in domestic arts, including gardening, cooking and sewing. Traditional educational subjects were a component of the Industrial School, as well. When the young ladies were "morally qualified" and a home could be found for them (either with their families or an adoptive one), the ladies were allowed to leave.

The school, started by the work of Laura Haviland, remained a landmark in the county until it closed in 2009.

BUSINESSES BEGIN

Returning soldiers often started new businesses when they came home after the war. A soldier's pay of $13 a month (in mid-1864, the pay was raised to $16 per month) made it easy for troops to save money. Additional bonuses for reenlisting of up to $500 were ready-made business financing for many.

In Hudson, the Thompson Savings Bank provides such an example. The Thompson brothers, Gamaliel, Royal and William, all served the Union cause during the Civil War. Only William enlisted, serving in the Eleventh Michigan Cavalry as a lieutenant colonel and a quartermaster for the unit. Gamaliel and Royal both operated as "independent contractors," working with the army in the field to fill out paperwork, manage supply chains and maintain transportation networks.

G.I. Thompson, one of the three Thompson brothers, who served in the war to raise funds to start what became the Thompson Savings Bank in Hudson. The bank was one of a handful of businesses and industries that came into being when soldiers returned home. *Courtesy of W.G. Thompson House Museum.*

The three brothers corresponded during the war. In the letters, the men agreed that they no longer wanted to work for anyone but themselves. They also agreed that Hudson was the place to return and open a business. The letters contained plans to open taverns and general stores; however, the men settled on opening a bank.

Saving their pay, the men returned to Hudson with over $2,000 each. With additional funding from friends and family, they attempted to open the bank in 1866 with $10,000 in capital. When the bank did not draw local investors and clients, they opened the business to a few more local investors. On November 9, 1867, the Perkins, Osborn and Company Bank opened.

The bank did well for all involved. By the 1880s, the investors were bought out, and the bank became known as the Thompson Brother's Banking House, later just Thompson Savings Bank. The bank was a pillar in the Hudson community until the third-generation president of the bank, William G. Thompson, sold it to United Bank and Trust of Tecumseh in 1999.

In Adrian, the woven wire fence industry grew out of one man who served during the Civil War. J. Wallace Page, who lived in Rollin Township prior to the war, enlisted in the Seventeenth Michigan when he was eighteen years old. His friends and family managed to convince Mr. Page to remain home from that enlistment.

In 1863, Page joined Battery F of the Michigan Light Artillery. Page would fight with Sherman outside Atlanta, defend Nashville from John Bell Hood and join Sherman in the final days of the war in North Carolina. Page was discharged on July 3, 1865.

When Page returned from the war, he spent the first afternoon at home in Rollin Township riding the mowing machine. Over the next few months, Page thought about how the armies used wood fence as firewood, as well as the destruction of woodlots throughout the South. Over the next twenty years, Page tinkered with weaving wire in his barn during quiet times.

With the assistance of his cousin Charles Lamb, Page perfected his wire loom machine and the method of making the knots in the weave. Finally, in 1889, Page incorporated the business. The Page Woven Wire Fence Company became a fixture in Adrian for over twenty years.

By 1902, the business was worth over $3 million and had its own ambassador baseball team of African American players and a park in Adrian with deer and other exotic animals to prove the worth of his fence. Page's idea spawned other fence factories in Adrian as well. Adrian soon became known as "the fence capital of the world."

A SPECIAL REUNION

One of the most interesting stories to come out of the service of Civil War soldiers in Lenawee County is the tale of Franklin Cobb of Hudson. Cobb attempted to enlist in Company F of the Fourth Michigan when war erupted. Finding that the regiment was full and there was no other space for him to enlist, Cobb jumped at the chance to qualify for the Berdan's Sharpshooters.

The Hudson men who served in Company C of the First U.S. Sharpshooters (Berdan's). *From left to right, back row*: Richard Wirts, Frank Cobb and Rupert Cooley; *front row*: Edward Southworth, Calvin Colwell and William Pomeroy. *Courtesy of Hudson Museum.*

Cobb easily qualified to join the First Regiment of Sharpshooters and paid his own way to Washington, D.C., to join the unit.

In May 1863, the First U.S. Sharpshooters took over guard duty for a section of Federal lines. The Pennsylvania regiment that was leaving told the sharpshooters to be careful of the Confederates, who seemed to shoot at everything. On the first day, the new men called over to the enemy lines inquiring of them why they shot at everything. The reply: "You commenced it."

When the Rebel troops found out that they were facing new men, they agreed to a truce in that section of lines. Friendships soon broke out as tobacco, newspapers and coffee were traded back and forth. In time, the men of Company C of the Sharpshooters and the Eleventh Alabama became friends. They agreed that should any of them be wounded in enemy lines, they would do what they could to aid one another.

The agreement was tested during the Battle of the Wilderness. Franklin Cobb would be shot through the right side. When Confederate troops overtook the area where Cobb lay, he asked what unit they were. The answer was the Eleventh Alabama. Cobb asked for William Sanders, the man with whom he had bartered in May of the previous year.

Frank Cobb (left) of the First U.S. Sharpshooters and William Sanders (right) of the Eleventh Alabama reunited fifty years after they met along the Rappahannock River. Sanders and his comrades saved Cobb's life at the Battle of the Wilderness. *Courtesy of Hudson Museum.*

Sanders brought three men with him to carry Cobb to a Confederate surgeon. Fearing the wound was fatal, the Confederates bid farewell to their friend. Cobb would lie in the field hospital in the Wilderness for a week before being transferred to a makeshift hospital in Lynchburg, Virginia. It took three months for him to recover in Lynchburg before he was transferred to Libby Prison. Eventually, he was paroled on September 12, 1864.

After the war ended, Franklin Cobb sent a letter to Alabama, asking if anyone recalled the episode during the Wilderness and, if they did, to contact him. Three responses came to Cobb, including one from William Sanders. The four men spent the next few decades corresponding about past events and current goings-on.

At the fiftieth anniversary of the Battle of Gettysburg, a reunion of Confederate and Union soldiers was held. Franklin Cobb and William Sanders both made the journey to the place they'd fought and were reunited. Cobb brought Sanders back to Hudson to stay for a few days before Sanders returned to Alabama.

Notes

Chapter 1

1. Letter, Ruth Evans to Jane Howell, October 22, 1832, Elizabeth Margaret Chandler Papers, Box 2, Folder 4, Call Number 85999. It should be noted that the membership of the society was not exclusively Quaker but included Presbyterians and Baptists.
2. Lindquist, *Antislavery*, 12
3. Laura Haviland, *Woman's Life Work* (Chicago: C.V. Waite & Company, 1887), 36.
4. Lindquist, *Antislavery*, 6–9.
5. McNaughton, *History of Adrian College*, 1–10.
6. Ibid., 10.
7. Haviland, *Woman's Life Work*, 52–90.
8. Lindquist, *Antislavery*, 62.

Chapter 2

9. Diary, Charles Cleveland, 1861, Cleveland Family Papers, Box 1, Call Number 85900.
10. Woodford, *Father Abraham's Children*, 35.
11. Ibid., 41.
12. Diary, Charles Cleveland.

13. Bertera and Crawford, *4th Michigan Infantry*, 14.
14. Watts, "Trial and Execution."
15. Account from the September 2, 1861 *Hudson Gazette.*

CHAPTER 3

16. Grimsley and Woodworth, *Shiloh*, 38.
17. Timothy T. Isbell, *Shiloh and Corinth: Sentinels of Stone* (Jackson: University of Mississippi Press, 2007), 35.
18. Bertera and Crawford, *4th Michigan Infantry*, 35.
19. *Hudson Gazette*, June 21, 1862.
20. Ibid., August 26, 1862.
21. Bertera and Crawford, *4th Michigan Infantry*, 81.
22. *Hudson Gazette*, September 20, 1862.
23. Bertera and Crawford, *4th MichiganInfantry*, 90–91.
24. Ibid., 91.
25. Ibid., 108.
26. Transcription of speech by Fernando Beaman in *Congressional Globe*, 37th Congress, 2nd Session, May 24, 1862, 204.
27. Bertera and Crawford, *4th Michigan Infantry*, 120.

CHAPTER 4

28. Faust, *11th Michigan*, 71.
29. Bertera, *DeGolyer's 8th Michigan*, 98.
30. Beyer and Keydel, *Deeds of Valor*, 176. Those men captured in action would be exchanged shortly before the fall of Vicksburg.
31. Bertera, *DeGolyer's 8th Michigan*, 129.
32. Bertera and Crawford, *4th Michigan Infantry*, 165.
33. Ibid., 167.
34. Ibid., 172.
35. Isham, *Seventh Michigan Cavalry*, 26.
36. Haviland, *Woman's Life Work*, 253.
37. Peter Cozzens, *This Terrible Sound* (Urbana, IL: University of Chicago Press, 1992), 258.
38. Ibid., 474.

39. An order from Union high command mandated that all new defensive structures be named after fallen officers with the rank of colonel or higher. When W.H. Smith was killed, a fort on the outskirts of Knoxville was named for him. Lorren Comstock would receive the same honor.
40. Dr. John Dawson, "Lenawee's Line of Splendor in the Civil War," Paper, January 14, 1987, Civil War Box 1, Lenawee County Historical Society Archives.

Chapter 5

41. Francis S. Dewey, "The Blizzard of '64 Vividly Described and Compared with the One We All Remember," *Onsted News*, 1918, https://lookaside.fbsbx.com/file/Great%20Blizzard%201864.pdf?token=AWyT6shZKzByG0XQcVV13SH7FoDBraYQTEX9nB6-6iFgQ6dnmRYUt6esBEL7xaDuXFffliVPxFabmUjwZ7ROgCysCmbs-7xjqlamEW58lZEjUA.
42. Saunier, *History*, 213.
43. Bertera and Crawford, *4th Michigan Infantry*, 198.
44. Report on the draft appeared in the November 11, 1863 edition of the *Tecumseh Herald*.
45. Rhea, *North Anna River*, 334.
46. Letter, Faron Anderson to brother, June 2, 1864, Faron Anderson Collection, Call Number 86999.
47. Bertera and Crawford, *4th Michigan Infantry*, 226.
48. Ibid., 227.
49. Ibid., 229.
50. Ibid., 206.
51. Faust, *11th Michigan*, 143.
52. Letter, Faron Anderson to mother, July 12, 1864, Faron Anderson Collection.
53. Letter, unknown soldier (possibly Clark?) to Mr. Anderson, August 3, 1864, Faron Anderson Collection. Anderson's family would locate the body and reinter Faron in Brookside Cemetery in Tecumseh.
54. Marshall, *Civil War Diary*, 34–35.

Chapter 6

55. Fred Ray, "Pre-Dawn Assault on Fort Steadman" *America's Civil War* (May 2005), http://www.civilwar.org/battlefields/petersburg/petersburg-history-articles/americas-civil-war-pre-dawn.html.

56. Diary, Charles Cleveland, March 28, 1865.
57. Ibid., March 31, 1865.
58. Watts, "Trial and Execution," 101–03.
59. Julian G. Dickinson, "The Capture of Jefferson Davis" (paper presented to the Military Order of the Loyal Legion of the United States on January 8, 1889, published 1899), http://suvcw.org/mollus/warpapers/MIv1p179.htm.
60. Ibid.
61. Newspaper clipping located in the Koon family file (n.d.), Hudson Museum.
62. Berry, *Loss of the* Sultana, 345–55.
63. *Adrian Weekly Times*, November 16, 1865
64. The July 6, 1866 edition of the *Adrian Daily Weekly* recounted the full text of the speech and the order of ceremony for the monument dedication.
65. James Malarney has produced an unpublished booklet, "The Lime Creek Thirty-Three." He estimates that there are over one hundred more soldiers from the area of Medina Township who perished during the war but are not on the marker, leading to his conclusion that the monument was funded privately by a group or by families.

Selected Bibliography

Barnett, LeRoy, and Roger Rosentreter. *Michigan's Early Military Forces*. Detroit, MI: Wayne State University Press, 2003.

Berry, Chester D. *Loss of the* Sultana *and Reminiscences of Survivors*. Lansing, MI: Darius D. Thorp Printer and Binder, 1892.

Bertera, Martin N. *DeGolyer's 8th Michigan Black Horse Light Battery*. Wyandotte, MI: TillieAnn Press, 2015.

Bertera, Martin N., and Kim Crawford. *The 4th Michigan Infantry in the Civil War*. East Lansing: Michigan State University Press, 2010.

Beyer, Walter F., and Oscar F. Keydel. *Deeds of Valor: How America's Heroes Won the Medal of Honor*. Detroit, MI: Perrien Keydel Company, 1901.

Brown, George H. *Record of Service of Michigan Volunteers in the Civil War, 1861–1865*. Vols. 1, 2, 4, 17, 18, 34, 37, 38, 41 Kalamazoo, MI: Ihling Brothers & Everard, 1900.

Bryant, William O. *Cahaba Prison and the* Sultana *Disaster*. Tuscaloosa: University of Alabama Press, 1990.

Catalogue of the Officers and Students of the Leoni Theological Institute, 1854–5. N.p.: Steam Printing establishment of R.F. Johnstone & Co., 1855.

Cleveland Family Papers. Bentley Historical Library.

Dempsey, Jack. *Michigan and the Civil War: A Great and Bloody Sacrifice*. Charleston, SC: The History Press, 2011.

Dempsey, Jack, and Brian Egan. *Michigan at Antietam: The Wolverine State's Sacrifice on America's Bloodiest Day*. Charleston, SC: The History Press, 2015.

Elizabeth Margret Chandler Papers. Bentley Historical Library.

Faron Anderson Papers. Bentley Historical Library

Faust, Eric R. *The 11th Michigan Volunteer Infantry in the Civil War: A History and Roster.* Jefferson, NC: McFarland & Company Inc., 2016.

Grimsley, Mark, and Steven E. Woodworth. *Shiloh: A Battlefield Guide.* Lincoln: University of Nebraska Press, 2006.

Hennessy, John. *The First Battle of Manassas: An End to Innocence July 18–21, 1861.* Lynchburg, VA: H.E. Howard Inc., 1989.

Isham, Asa B. *Seventh Michigan Cavalry of Custer's Wolverine Brigade.* Huntington, WV: Blue Acorn Press, 2000.

Jass, Stephanie. *No Victory without Work: A Pictorial History of Adrian College.* Virginia Beach, VA: Downing Company Publishers, 2009.

Lindquist, Charles. *The Antislavery-Underground Railroad Movement in Lenawee County, Michigan 1830–1860.* Adrian, MI: Lenawee County Historical Society, Inc., 1990.

———. *Spanning the Years: A History of Blissfield, Michigan, 1824–1999.* Adrian, MI: Lenawee County Historical Society, Inc., 2000.

Lindquist, Charles N., Frederick G. Eaton and Mary Ward-Eaton. *Lenawee County: A Harvest of Pride and Promise: An Illustrated History.* Chatsworth, CA: Windsor Publications, 1990.

Marshall, William H. *Civil War Diary.* N.p.: Estate of William Harrison Marshall, 2008.

McNaughton, A. Douglas. *A History of Adrian College.* Adrian, MI: Adrian College, 1994.

Mull, Carol E. *The Underground Railroad in Michigan.* Jefferson, NC: McFarland and Company, Inc., Publishers, 2010.

Rhea, Gordon. *To the North Anna River: Grant and Lee May 13–25, 1864.* Baton Rouge, LA: LSU Press, 2005.

Robertson, John, comp. *Michigan in the War.* Lansing, MI: W.S. George & Company State Printers and Binders, 1882.

Saunier, Joseph A. *A History of the Forty-seventh Regiment, Ohio Veteran Volunteer Infantry.* Hillsboro, OH: Lyle Printing Co., 1903.

Schmutz, John F. *The Battle of the Crater: A Complete History.* Jefferson, NC: McFarland and Company, Inc., Publishers, 2009.

Scott, Robert Garth. *Into the Wilderness with the Army of the Potomac.* Bloomington: Indiana University Press, 1988.

Waldron, Clara. *One Hundred Years a Country Town: The Village of Tecumseh, Michigan, 1824–1924.* Tecumseh, MI: Thomas A. Riordan, 1968.

Watts, Richard A. "The Trial and Execution of the Lincoln Conspirators." *Michigan History* 6 (1922): 81–110.

Woodford, Frank B. *Father Abraham's Children: Michigan Episodes in the Civil War.* Detroit, MI: Wayne State University Press, 1961.

Index

V

W

About the Author

Ray Lennard is curator at the William G. Thompson House Museum and Gardens in Hudson, Michigan. Mr. Lennard is a graduate of Adrian College and the School of Information at the University of Michigan. He is president of the Lenawee County Civil War Roundtable, has served on the board of directors of the Lenawee County Historical Society and is a longtime Civil War reenactor. He resides in Adrian with his wife, Kara, and four rambunctious Cardigan Welsh corgis.

Visit us at
www.historypress.net

This title is also available as an e-book